Servant First!

Leadership for the
New Millennium

John J. Sullivan

PRESS

Dedication

This book is dedicated to Jeanne Phyllis Gapp Sullivan and Roberta Randall Rice Sullivan, two women who have lived their lives as Servants First, but especially to the Carpenter from Nazareth who set the example for future leaders by the life He led.

Paul Johnson ("An 'Ism' for All Seasons," National Review, October 13, 2003) has observed that, at the beginning of the new millennium, discontented intellectuals, the media, and those who seek a utopia on earth have embraced the ideology of pessimism. We can do nothing in the face of economic stagnation, business corruption, global warming, and international terrorism, according to the habit of mind of the pessimists. But, there is a viable alternative—the optimism of those who can adopt the leadership example set by Jesus Christ to serve others. John Sullivan's Servant First: Leadership for the New Millennium sets forth this optimistic alternative in a lucid and practical manner. Drawing from recent scholarship on management and leadership, especially Deming's total quality management and Greenleaf's servant leadership, his own diverse experience as a leader, and biblical examples, Sullivan develops a practical model for Christian leadership. The concluding chapters provide numerous examples showing how a person who adopts the nature of a servant leader, applying the principles and behaviors exemplified by Christ, can lead well. This book thus presents a positive alternative for anyone interested in moving away from the naysayers toward a culture of personal, corporate, and societal optimism.

J. Thomas Whetstone, D.Phil.
Associate Professor of Business & Philosophy
Montreat College
Montreat, NC 28757
15 October 2003

Preface

This book was conceived in 1995 when I developed a course at Montreat College called *Servant Leadership*. I had become fascinated with the idea of leaders serving others beginning back in the late 1980s, when I ran across Tom Peters' books on excellent organizations (see Chapter 4 for a more compete discussion). Peter's led me to Deming, and Deming to many other proponents of the quality movement. I read everything I could get my hands on about quality management since it made so much sense to me. From 1987 to 1990, I commanded a Marine Corps air station and was able to put into practice the approach and techniques I had been studying.

In 1990, I was assigned as a professor of management at the Naval War College, Newport, RI. There I continued my research, writing and teaching on quality and became active in the budding State quality effort. I helped write the State quality award, was one of their first lead examiners, and did some consulting in the private and public sectors.

When I accepted a teaching position at Montreat College, one of the things that attracted me was their stated objective of educating "servant leaders." Although the College had several yearly activities associated with servant leadership, these primarily involved invited outside speakers and service opportunities for the students. Since they did not have a formal course in the catalog, I decided to develop one. As I began researching servant leadership, I found Robert Greenleaf's writings to be helpful. I was struck by the compatibility between Greenleaf's servant leadership and the philosophy of quality management. I saw how the concept of leader as servant fit with the tools and techniques of quality management. Yet I sensed that Greenleaf's model lacked something. Then I discovered that the model for servant as leader was right before me!

No other leader in the history of the world has so lived out the philosophy of servant leadership than Jesus of Nazareth. As I studied the life of Jesus *from a leadership perspective*, I discovered that He had a set of guiding principles, a strategy, plans, tactics and a revolutionary way of dealing with people. He *was* the ultimate servant leader and that was the missing element.

In developing the course, I read everything I could get my hands on dealing with leadership. Much written today on the subject of leadership seems to be articulating the blindingly obvious. However, there are some very good sources for students of leadership and many of them were used in the preparation of this book. In the chapters on traditional leadership theories, I have tried to find common ground among the various theories so as to make them more easily comprehensible. I have broken the various theories into three groups: leader-focused, follower-focused, and situation-focused. Obviously, I have not dealt in depth with any of the major theories and I have not referenced others. However, I believe that I have adequately laid the groundwork for comparison with servant leadership, which was my intent.

I include two chapters on quality leadership not only due to my own interest in the subject but also because I don't see the quality philosophy receiving the credit it is due in transforming the way modern businesses are led and managed.

Fascinating to me was the Hawthorne Effect connection in helping to shape the leadership philosophy of a young W. Edwards Deming (see Chapter 4).

Greenleaf's approach to servant leadership is addressed in two chapters along with my own interpretation of his leadership philosophy. I include a chapter on Christian leadership drawn extensively from George Barna's book, *The Second Coming of the Church*. Barna is founder and president of Barna Research Group. Based on nearly twenty years of research, he sounds a cautionary warning for leaders of the Christian church in America today. Although his book is aimed at church leaders, I believe he has identified elements, competencies, traits, and leader types that resonate with servant leaders.

The next seven chapters of the book are devoted to peeling back the layers of the onion and discovering Jesus as servant leader. Most of this research is from a direct study of the New Testament, specifically the life of Jesus as depicted in the gospels of Matthew, Mark, Luke, and John. There are other books available on the subject of Jesus as leader but I did not find any that attempted to take a comprehensive look at how Jesus created an "organization" that has successfully grown over the past two thousand years with a servant as leader philosophy. I am not a theologian and I have tried to avoid any discussion of theology. I hope the reader will agree. My purpose was not to convince anyone of the deity of Jesus for that is a matter between each reader and the Almighty. Rather, I have tried to dissect the rather remarkable leadership philosophy of that itinerate rabbi who refused to use power for His own ends and called his followers to a life of service to others.

The book concludes with profiles of two leaders who have applied the concept of servant leadership in the not-for-profit and the for-profit sectors.

A Disclaimer

Some of you may get a little hot under the collar with any suggestion that Jesus may be compared to *any* human being or that any "organization" He created could be duplicated by men and women. After all, Jesus is divine, God Himself! How can mortal man hope to follow His leadership example? As a disciple of the Carpenter, I acknowledge Jesus as LORD and confess that while He was in this "earthly tent" He was fully man yet fully God (Hebrews 2:14). As a man, He was confined to a human body and voluntarily gave up some of His divine power in order to be fully human. He said that He did not come to abolish the law but to fulfill it (Matthew 5:17).

The Ten Commandments, written by God and delivered to us through the Jews, are divided into laws dealing with man's relationship with God (1-4), and man's relationship with each other (5-10) (Exodus 20:1-17). Jesus' teaching included both types of instruction. He spent considerable time explaining how we are to live with one another in families, communities, and nations. Jesus used many teaching methods including modeling the behavior He expected His disciples to follow. He said, "He who has seen Me has seen the Father" (John 14:9). Therefore the behaviors that Jesus taught and modeled were from God Himself *including how He led others*. If we acknowledge that His teaching about our relationship with God and with other men and women is valid, why would we not also acknowledge that his teaching about leadership is equally valid? Just as He has taught us how to live in relation to Him and each other, so God has taught us how to lead—by being a servant first! I believe that the model He lived out for us as a leader may be studied and applied to all types of organizations and that is what this book aims to show.

Contents

1

Servant as Leader?

*"... but whoever wants to become great among you must
be your servant, and whoever wants to be first must be your
slave—just as the Son of Man did not come to be served,
but to serve, and to give His life as a ransom for many."*
—*Matthew 20:26b-28*

Servant leadership?

Servant leadership. The term appears paradoxical. How
can someone be a servant and yet a leader? Even if you
could possibly be both, how is the concept relevant to leaders today? It's a nice, fuzzy concept that might work in
churches and some non-profits but not elsewhere and surely
not in the rough and tumble world of business! No way!

Those are typical reactions to the term "servant leadership." Certainly, this mindset seemed to impact the leadership
of men like Lincoln, Gandhi, King, and others but is it appropriate for today? Much has been written about the concept of

servant as leader but it remains misunderstood as a vibrant, effective leadership approach for business. This book will explore the paradox of servant as leader and show how this approach to leadership *is* effective and relevant for men and women in the church and para-church organizations but also in the public and for-profit and not-for-profit sectors.

Our journey begins with a quick review of the major traditional and historical approaches to leadership theory. Next we will examine the contributions of the quality revolution to the study of leadership. We will explore servant leadership as defined by Robert K. Greenleaf, a Quaker businessman who popularized the term "servant leader." Then, we will look at some unique requirements for leaders in Christian organizations. With this foundation, we will turn to an examination of the leadership style of Jesus of Nazareth. We will discover the radical, unconventional leadership approach of Jesus by examining his strategy, guiding principles, traits and behaviors, and tactics that mark his distinctive leadership style. We conclude with profiles of contemporary leaders who have successfully applied the concept of servant first.

Why pick Jesus as a model for leadership? Jesus was able to create an "organization" using a very unlikely group of followers that has endured for over two millennia and has continued to grow worldwide in spite of fierce opposition, persecution, and even martyrdom for its members. One author writes:

> One person trained twelve human beings who went on to so influence the world that time itself is now recorded as being before or after his existence.
>
> This person worked with a staff that was totally human and not divine...a staff that in

spite of illiteracy, questionable background, fractious feelings, and momentary cowardice went on to accomplish the tasks he trained them to do.

They did this for one main reason—to be with him again (Jones 1995).

Misconceptions about leadership

Before we begin our discussion, let's address several common misconceptions about leaders and leadership.

A student in a seminar for new team leaders that I was teaching asked me, "Does this mean that I don't have to have all the answers?" This first-level supervisor was relieved to know that with a team approach to leadership he alone did not have to come up with the solutions to problems and make the right decisions. As we are seeing in many organizations today, *leadership is collective*, i.e., it is shared between the leader and her followers. A leader of a small office or branch is able to reach out and connect with her followers on a daily basis. She is generally expert in all of the functions of that office. However, as this leader moves up the ladder, she is no longer able to reach out to each person in her organization on a daily basis and she is probably no longer expert in all the functions that she commands. It is ironic that as we assume more responsibility we become *more* dependent upon our followers.

Similarly, *influence works both ways*: up the chain of command as well as down. A subordinate with a high level of expertise (e.g., how to use the new software program) or someone having a personal relationship with a senior decision maker can exert tremendous influence on critical outcomes. As a Department of the Navy aviation program coordinator in the Pentagon in the 1980's, I soon discovered that if I wanted to get a favorable decision from the Secretary of the Navy affecting my program, I first had to get the endorsement of his assistant who had an obscure office buried in that five-sided building. This man's name did not even appear on the organizational chart for the Department of the Navy staff. However, he was an old friend of the Secretary's and was charged by him with reviewing all aviation program proposals. His was a classic case of referent power (i.e., his power came from his relationship to the Secretary of the Navy). Leaders influence followers but followers influence leaders, too.

Leadership is simply exercising good common sense, right? Hopefully, leaders do exercise common sense but can "rules of thumb" solve every problem in the workplace? What rule of thumb should I use when my boss tells me we have to cut our workforce by 25%? Do I use "first in last out," or "last in first out?" What if the last person I hired was a gifted and hard-working single mom with two small children to feed? Often, our common sense rules of thumb do not work when dealing with people with different skills, ambitions, and needs. Leadership is much more than just common sense.

Leaders are born not made.[1] Proponents of this theory argue that some people are simply born to lead and some are born to follow. It's nature over nurture. Therefore, nothing is to be gained by the study of leadership because either you've got it or you don't! This is the argument for the study of traits or characteristics of the "Great Captains" or great leaders. One simply has to identify those who have these desirable traits and you've found your future leaders. As we'll see when we look at the trait theories, this approach does not hold water, either. The problem with this approach is that researchers were not able to identify a set of traits that were common to all successful leaders (Stogdill 1974). Recent studies have suggested that there may be a few traits common to successful leaders but those same traits may be found in non-leaders as well (Bennis 1992; Conger 1991; Bass 1985; Kouzes and Posner 1993). Most people can learn to lead. Some will augment their natural, God-given talents with drive, determination, and dedication to become great leaders. However, these are a small percentage of leaders; most men and women who want to learn how to lead can do so with success.

Finally, some argue that *we learn only from the school of hard knocks*. This myth would have us believe that experience is our only worthy teacher. The result of this approach is reactive leadership. One can never be proactive, according to this misconception. Conversely, is the formal study of leadership exclusive of learning from experience? Certainly not! As a young officer in the U.S. Marine Corps, I carried a small notebook that contained notes on the behaviors and actions of the leaders I observed. Most of these were negative: I'll never make *that* mistake! But some of them were positive: what a great way to recognize someone's accomplishments! I was learning from experience: the experience of others. Now it is certainly true we learn from our own experience, but a wise leader will prepare himself for positions of leadership through formal study as well as from his experiences.

Leadership or management?

Ten-year-old Chase slipped in to the back of the room just as my Principles of Management class began. He was accompanying his brother, a high school senior, who was visiting our college campus along with his parents, my wife's cousins. The discussion that day dealt, in part, with leadership and management. I posed the question, "What are the differences between leadership and management?" After some thoughtful discussion among the first- and second-year students, we moved on to other topics. When the class ended, Chase came to the front of the classroom where I was packing up my things and declared, "How basic! Even I know the difference between leadership and management. Leaders lead and managers manage." Just so! But let's try to breakdown the responsibilities and characteristics of each.

Leadership and management are *complimentary* functions: they are not one in the same. Leaders are responsible for *effectiveness*; managers for *efficiency*. Another way of saying this is: leaders do the right *things*; managers do things *right*. Stephen Covey suggests that we manage from the left and lead from the right (brain) (Covey 1989).

International Business Machine was one of the most successful firms ever created and yet Big Blue nearly lost it all in the early 1990's not because they weren't building a superior product, they were! They built the best mainframe computers money could buy. The problem was customers wanted desktop personal computers. The senior leadership of IBM did not recognize this shift in customer preferences until it was nearly too late. The result was a clean sweep of senior management and massive layoffs—the first in the history of IBM. The IBM people were building a superior product using the best manufacturing techniques, quality and cost control. They were doing things right. They were very efficient. The problem was senior leadership had become complacent and had lost their vision for the future. They were *not* doing the right things.

Figure 1.1 contrasts some of the differences between leaders and managers.

Figure 1.1

Differences: Leaders and Managers

- Leaders innovate; managers administer
- Leaders develop; managers maintain
- Leaders inspire; managers control
- Leaders take a long view; managers a short view
- Leaders ask "what" and "why"; managers ask "how" and "when"
- Leaders originate; mangers imitate
- Leaders challenge the status quo; managers accept it

Adapted from Genevieve Capowski, "Anatomy of a Leader: Where Are the Leaders of Tomorrow?" *Management Review,* March 1994, p. 12

We now turn our attention to the traditional approaches to leadership theory.

Endnote

[1] The last two "myths" are adapted from Hughes, Ginnett and Curphy (1993)

2

Traditional Models
of Leadership

*"Use power to help people. For we are given power not to
advance our own purposes nor to make a great show in the
world, nor a name. There is but one just use of power
and it is to serve people."*
—Former President George H. W. Bush

Overview

What is leadership? J. Oswald Sanders defined leadership as influence, "the ability of one person to influence others to follow his or her lead" (1994, 27). Dwight David Eisenhower, defined leadership as the art of getting someone else to do something you want done because he wants to do it! A more formal definition of leadership has it as the process of influencing an organized group toward accomplishing its goals (Roach and Behling 1984). The study of leadership—or why some leaders are successful and others are not—can be traced to the industrial revolution and the end of the nineteenth century. Leadership involves three elements: a leader, followers, and a situation. Likewise, the study of leadership focused first on the leader, then on his relationship with followers, and finally on situational variables.

> *"True greatness, true leadership, is found in giving yourself in service to others, not in coaxing or inducing others to serve you."*
> —*J. Oswald Sanders*

The trait (or characteristics) approach, the behavior approach, and the situational (or contingency) approach to leadership each has contributed to the understanding of leadership but none is exhaustive in explaining the art and science of leadership. More recently, the quality revolution has had a profound impact on leadership theory and behavior.

However, these approaches fail to fully address the intrinsic motivational aspect of leadership, i.e., what is the driving force that makes a person want to lead? What is a leader's fundamental motivation for decisions? This is where servant leadership differs from all other approaches to leadership. After discussing traditional leadership theory and the contributions from the quality revolution, I will explain how servant leadership is radically different from these other approaches.

Trait Studies: Focus on the Leader

Early leadership studies focused on the traits of the leader. This research dominated the leadership studies in the late nineteenth and early twentieth century. The belief that leaders are born not made, and that the discovery of the personality, values and characteristics of the great men of history would reveal their secrets dominated research on leadership (Carlyle [1841] 1907, James 1880, Galton 1869). After over forty years of research, there is very little evidence to justify the assertion that leaders are born with some identifiable set of traits that sets them apart from followers (Ackerson 1942; Bird 1940; Jenkins 1947; Stogdill 1948). There is strong evidence to suggest that on average leaders are more sociable, more aggressive, more lively, more original, more popular, and have a better sense of humor than group members. However which of these traits are most relevant seems to depend on the requirements of the situation. In other words, having a combination of these traits does not guarantee that a person will become an effective leader (Nahavandi 2000).

> *"In reading the lives of great men, I found that the first victory they won was over themselves...self-discipline with all of them came first."*
> —*Former President Harry S. Truman*

More recent studies have suggested that factors such as intelligence (Bray and Grant 1966) or assertiveness (Rychlak 1963) have some relationship to leadership but they alone cannot account for a leader's effectiveness. However, as we will see in Chapter 6, Robert Greenleaf asserts that servant leaders do have an identifiable set of traits that set them apart from their followers (Greenleaf 1991).

A study of several hundred U.S. Army General Officers from World War II concluded that leaders are made not born (Puryear 1971). Some of these senior officers believed that leadership characteristics were important but that they were not enough to guarantee a person would be a good leader. General Carl "Tooey" Spaatz observed, "I think you must be born with certain characteristics, but it's more a case of what takes place after you are born that decides whether or not you are going to be a leader" (Puryear 1971, xi). Perhaps General William H. Simpson best summed up the conclusions of these officers when he said, "Everyone is not a born leader. Leadership can be learned. The successful handling of men requires the application of certain qualities of leadership. There are few natural leaders, very few" (Puryear 1971, xii).

Research on leadership traits continues. A recent study on public leadership identified six key qualities or abilities as most important for leaders in pubic life: ability to inspire; excellent people skills; personal direction; understanding of authority and power; synergy with followers; and, an ethical orientation (Goodman 2000). The author cautions that mastery of these abilities does not necessarily assure effective leadership.

> *"All great leaders have one common spiritual gift—faith."*
> —*Elmer Towns*

Behavior Studies: Focus on the Followers

Several factors during the mid-1940's led researchers to examine the observable behaviors of leaders as the source of leadership effectiveness. The failure of the trait approach and the need to train leaders for service in World War II led researchers toward emphasizing *what* an effective leader does rather than *who* would be an effective leader.

Behaviorist theories were gaining dominance at this

same time, particularly in the United States and Great Britain (Nahavandi 2000). Focusing on behaviors provided several advantages over the trait approaches for researchers:

- Behaviors can be observed more objectively than traits
- Behaviors can be measured more precisely than traits
- Behaviors can be taught (Nahavandi 2000)

> "We have different gifts, according to the grace given us. If a man's gift is ... leadership, let him govern diligently."
> —Romans 12:6-8

These factors provided a clear benefit to the military and other organizations interested in leadership. Instead of identifying people with certain personality traits, they could focus on training people to perform effective leadership behaviors.

The first of these behavioral studies focused on how the leader makes decisions. Lewin and his associates (Lewin and Lippit 1938; Lewin, Lippit, and White 1939) placed leaders on a continuum as depicted below.

Autocratic ◄————————————► Laissez-faire

Autocratic leaders were defined as making decisions without input from their followers. *Laissez-faire* leaders provided minimal direction to followers and had little or no involvement with decision-making. Between these two extremes was the *democratic* leader who consulted followers and allowed them to participate in decision-making.

Subsequent studies expanded the list of observed behaviors to better identify successful leader styles. These studies may be characterized as *follower-focused*. These studies examined the leader's interaction with followers over a wide variety of behaviors and placed leaders on another continuum:

Job-focused ⟵——————————⟶ People-focused

The Ohio State studies (Hemphill 1949) measured leader behaviors in actual work settings. They concluded that leaders could be described in terms of two primary dimensions of behavior:

- *Consideration* (friendly and supportive toward subordinates)
- *Initiating structure* (emphasis on meeting goals and accomplishing tasks)

Studies at the University of Michigan built on the earlier Ohio State research but rather than describe a variety of exhibited behavior, they tried to identify behaviors that contributed to effective group performance (Likert 1961). They placed these behaviors in two categories:

- *Job-centered dimensions* (goal emphasis, work facilitation)
- *Employee-centered* (leaders support, interaction facilitator)

These two categories may be compared to the Ohio State studies:

- *Initiating structure = Job-centered*
- *Consideration = Employee-centered*

In other words, leaders were classified as focusing on the needs of their followers (people-centered) or focusing on job accomplishment (mission-centered). They concluded that leaders who were more people-centered tended to have more satisfied employees. However, when faced with difficult and ambiguous tasks, leaders who were mission-centered exhibited higher performance.

The Situational Leadership Model—discussed in the next chapter—is a more recent conceptualization of leadership styles following on the University of Michigan and Ohio State studies (Blake and McCanse 1991). The Model profiles leader behaviors on two dimensions: *concern for people* (supportive behavior) and *concern for production* (directive behavior). The Model suggests that leaders are not limited to an either-or style (i.e., autocratic or democratic) but may move around the grid based on "a unique set of assumptions for using power and authority to link people to production" (Blake and McCanse 1991, 29).

At about the same time as the University of Michigan studies, Douglas McGregor (1966) attempted to explain different styles of leadership on the basis of the leader's attitudes about human nature. These two contrasting sets of assumptions people make about human nature he called *Theory X* and *Theory Y*. Theory X leaders take a pessimistic view of human nature and believe that followers must be motivated by extrinsic, coercive means or they will not perform. While Theory Y leaders believe that most people are trustworthy and are intrinsically motivated by their work. Theory Y leaders believe that their responsibilities are to provide the resources needed for their followers to perform at high levels.

> *"Trust men and they will be true to*
> *you; treat them greatly and they will*
> *show themselves great."*
> —*Ralph Waldo Emerson*

James McGregor Burns (1978), building on earlier behavioral studies, identified a leadership style he called *transformational leadership.* Up to this time, Burns argued, leadership studies had focused on leadership as an "exchange process." That is, leaders established a *transactional* relationship with followers that promised certain rewards in exchange for performance. Burns declared that leadership, as a transaction must give way to a higher order of change—to transformational leadership. Transformational leaders motivate followers to transcend their personal needs and set the needs of the group above their own.

> *True leadership must be for the benefit*
> *of the followers, not the enrichment of*
> *the leaders.*
> —*Anonymous*

We may summarize these behavior studies by characterizing *people-centered* leadership to include participative (democratic) leadership, team leadership, Theory Y leaders, and transformational leaders. *Mission-centered* leadership would include autocratic leaders, Theory X leaders, and transactional leaders. People-centered leaders use power to help their followers grow, to provide them the resources they need and to develop them to become leaders themselves. Mission-centered leaders use power to achieve goals and mission success but also to meet their own needs.

In the next chapter, we'll look at leadership research focused not on the leader or the followers but on the situation.

3

Situational Leadership®

I know, my God, that you test the heart and are pleased with integrity.
—1 Chronicles 29:17a

Situational Leadership: Focus on the Situation[a]

Finally, *Situational Leadership®* studies examined the changing conditions within a given situation (people/ task) and concluded that leaders must either be placed in a situation that fits their leadership style or change their style as the situation dictates. It is true that leaders do not interact with all followers in the same manner. People must be led one person at a time. Some early studies in Situational Leadership® postulated that leaders have a certain style and that in order to be successful, they must be placed in a situation that fits their style of leadership (Fiedler 1967). This theory fails to account for the realization that all situations (and people) change and therefore a leadership style that was appropriate for a given time and place may no longer be appropriate over time.

Hersey and Blanchard (1969, 1977, 1982, 2001) developed Situational Leadership® theory to help explain an optimum style for leaders given different followers and missions. Unlike Fiedler, they argued that a leader could and should change his style based on situational factors. Their research built on the Ohio State studies but they renamed their behavior categories: *task behaviors* (initiating structure) and *relationship behaviors* (consideration). Four leadership styles emerged: *telling* (high task, low relationship), *selling* (high task, high relationship), *participating* (low task, high relationship), and *delegating* (low task, low relationship) (see Figure 3-1). These four combinations of task and relationship behaviors were contingent on the ability and willingness of followers to complete a task, or what they termed *follower readiness* (Hughes, Blanchard, and Johnson 2001). Follower readiness was composed of two components: ability and willingness, or what I prefer to call *competence* and *commitment*.

Competence is a task-specific component and will therefore vary from one function or task to the next. Commitment, however, is global; i.e., you are committed to the mission and vision of the organization or you are not. Commitment is not necessarily related to task although task may have an impact on the strength of commitment. The Situational Leadership® Model further segmented follower readiness into four levels from low to high readiness. To use the model, leaders should first assess the readiness level of a follower (competence and commitment). Next, a vertical line is drawn from the center of the readiness level up to the point where it intersects with the bell-shaped curve in Figure 3-1. The quadrant in which this intersection occurs represents the level of task and relationship behavior that has the best chance of producing successful outcomes (Hughes, Ginnett, and Curphy 1993).

Figure 3-1 Situational Leadership® Model

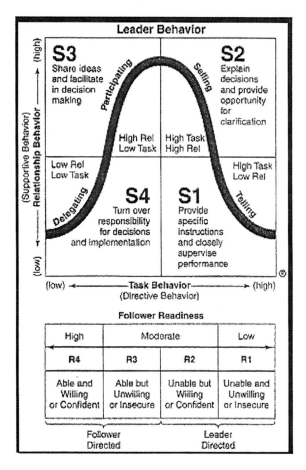

SOURCE: Adapted from Paul Hersey, Kenneth H. Blanchard, and Dewey E. Johnson, *Management of Organizational Behavior, Leading Human Resources, 8th Ed* (Upper Saddle River, NJ: Prentice Hall, 2001), p. 182. Reprinted with permission of Center for Leadership Studies, Inc. Escondido, CA.

> *"Whatever you have learned or received or heard from me, or seen in me—put into practice."*
> —*Philippians 4:9*

How would this apply in a real work setting? Imagine yourself as a newly assigned supervisor of a manufacturing branch with 30 employees. Over your first few weeks on the job you make an assessment of the work to be done and the competence and commitment of the people assigned to do it. For example, let's say that Harry Jones has been a machine operator for about six months. As you've gotten to know him you have found out that he is attending college classes at night and plans on getting a degree in business within the next two years. His dream is to be a plant manager one day. He is committed to the mission and vision of the firm. You assess his maturity level as high in commitment but low in competence. Hersey and Blanchard would probably place him in the S2 category. I would lead him by being more prescriptive (selling) with task-specific responsibilities while creating situations where he can grow (participating, delegating) in other non-task related areas.

In another example, Mary Smith is an experienced salesperson with good marketing skills but she struggles with record keeping. Word on the grapevine is that she is actively looking for a sales position in another company. Your assessment of her competence level is high for sales but low for record keeping. You have reason to suspect her commitment to the organization is low. How would you lead this woman? Do you need to be more directive and provide closer control until she improves her accounting skills? That might appear to be the optimum approach but it is probably just what she doesn't need! Why is Ms. Smith looking for another job? When you find the answer to that question you may discover that she: (1) is frustrated that she is not able to keep accurate, timely records; (2) would like training in accounting; and (3) either has asked for help and none was provided, or is afraid to ask for help. She is running away from the problem. Your job as her leader is to provide her the training she needs so that she can perform at a high level in all of her assigned tasks.

Situational leadership means that your leadership style must change as the situation changes. As people mature or are replaced by new employees, a leader must adjust his style to the changing circumstances. Let me illustrate this concept using terms from my fighter pilot background. When a fighter crew is running an intercept on another aircraft under the radar control of a tactical air controller, the term is *"close control."* However, when the situation becomes so dynamic that the ground-based controller is unable to manage each movement (heading, airspeed, altitude) of the airborne fighter aircraft, he will issue *"bulls-eye"* information. That is, the controller turns over management of the intercept to the fighter crews and simply provides information (distance, heading, airspeed, and altitude) on the other aircraft from a known geographical location. The pilots in the "arena" may take independent action to accomplish their mission. Let me illustrate with a true story.

A few weeks after I assumed command of a military installation some years ago, I asked the officer responsible for the purchase of equipment, "How many computers and printers do we have on this base?" He was unable to readily provide the answer. At that point, I ordered him to stop all requisitions of computer equipment (hardware and software) and to conduct a wall-to-wall inventory. I had lost confidence in his ability to control an important function that had been delegated to him. I decided to close-control that function. When he provided me with an inventory record some weeks later, I spot-checked several pieces of equipment against the inventory and found some errors. I returned the inventory and told him to do it again.

Several weeks later, I received a second inventory that, when I spot-checked, proved to be accurate. Now I told the supply officer that he could begin accepting orders for computer equipment but that each order must be accompanied by written justification for the purchase. I further told him to create a small team of experts who would perform an on-site evaluation of each request and to make a recommendation to him as to whether the requested equipment or software was justified. He, in turn, would forward to me those requests that he felt were justified. By now, six months had elapsed. I let this system work for another six months until I was satisfied that the supply officer had demonstrated the competency required to assume responsibility for this important purchasing function.

Twelve months from the time I asked for the first inventory, I called the supply officer to my office and said, "I have reviewed all of your recommendations for computer equipment purchases over the last six months and I am convinced that you are able to control this important function. Therefore, I am delegating this responsibility to you. You will now make the purchasing decisions." As I became convinced of his competence, I moved from close-control to bulls-eye. I continued to periodically review computer purchases over the next couple of years and I never had to close-control this officer again.

In the last two chapters, we have reviewed the major traditional leadership theories:
- Leader-focused (traits)
- Follower-focused (behaviors)
- Situation-focused

Leader-focused theories tried to identify a set of traits or characteristics that distinguished leaders from followers. This approach failed to justify the assertion that leaders are born with some identifiable set of traits that sets them apart from followers. Recent studies have identified some common traits of leaders but they have failed to be predictive of successful leaders.

Follower-focused theories examined the relationships between leaders and followers in a variety of observed behaviors. The first of these studies focused on how the leader makes decisions. They identified leadership style on a continuum from autocratic to laissez-faire. Subsequent studies expanded the list of observed behaviors to better identify successful leader styles. Although the terms used have slight variation, these studies place leaders on a continuum from mission-centered to people-centered.

Finally, situational leadership studies concluded that leaders must evaluate the people and the task at hand and tailor their style to the situation. As the situation (people/task) changes, so must a leader's style.

Now that we've reviewed some of the traditional approaches to leadership, we turn to the contributions that the quality revolution has made to the art and science of leadership.

4

Quality Leadership

*"Total Quality represents the century's most profound,
comprehensive alteration in management theory
and practice."*
—*Stephen R. Covey*

Often overlooked in the leadership literature are the contributions to modern leadership theory brought about through the quality revolution during the last two decades of the twentieth century. Total quality management was a program developed in Japan within the last decade and imported to America, right? Wrong on all four counts! I'll explain why in the following pages.

Background and History

My own journey to quality began in the late 1980s when I read Peters' and Waterman's book, *In Search of Excellence: Lessons from America's Best-Run Companies* (1982). I remember thinking, "There are a lot of good ideas and principles here that I can use in my organization!" Although Peters was writing primarily about for-profit companies, I could see that the principles would apply to not-for-profits too. As I began to read more on the subject of excellence in products and service, I discovered Dr. Deming.

William Edwards Deming, the prophet of the quality revolution, like Moses, rose to national prominence at age 80. Born at the turn of the century in Sioux City, Iowa, this physicist/statistician became the herald for a "new" style of leadership. His *14 Points for Management* evolved over the years from the use of statistical methods into a full-blown guide to management (Walton 1990). To understand how his leadership theory evolved, let's look at a brief biography of Deming and his mentor, Walter Shewhart.

Walter A. Shewhart was an engineer with the Western Electric Company of Chicago, maker of Bell telephones, and later at the Bell Telephone Laboratories in New York, from 1918 to 1956. Shewhart brought together the disciplines of statistics, engineering, and economics and became known as the father of modern quality control (Ott 1967). He is most widely known today for his development of the control chart, a simple but highly effective tool that separated common cause process variation from special cause variation. To Deming he was simply "the master" (Deming 1982). His genius, Deming would say, was in recognizing when to act and when to leave a process alone (Walton 1986).

Deming grew up in the Wild West frontier towns of Cody and later, Powell, Wyoming. He graduated from the University of Wyoming in 1921 and taught at the university for another year before enrolling in a master's program in mathematics and physics at the University of Colorado. In 1924, he was encouraged by a professor to continue his studies at Yale. He got his PhD in physics there three years later. During his summers while a graduate student at Yale, he worked on transmitters at Western Electric's Hawthorne plant in Chicago. In 1927, he turned down job offers in private enterprise to work for the U.S. Department of Agriculture in the fixed nitrogen laboratory. While he was there, a colleague introduced him to Walter Shewhart. For several years, Deming would travel to New York to study with Shewhart (Walton 1986). Another of the bright young protégées of Shewhart during this time was Joseph Juran. Fifty years later, these two octogenarians, Deming and Juran, would lead the quality revolution in Asia, North America and Europe.

In 1942, soon after the United States had entered World War II, Dr. Deming, then an advisor in sampling with the Bureau of the Census, was asked by a consultant to the Secretary of War for ideas on ways to aid the war effort. Deming suggested a short course in Shewhart methods to teach the basics of applied statistics to engineers and managers (American Society for Quality 2000).

The short courses on applied statistics were repeated many times over the next several years during WWII and they laid the foundation for the statistical quality control movement in the U.S. No doubt the quality systems developed in American industry as a result of these courses made a significant contribution to the high rate of war materials production. This is especially noteworthy considering the largely inexperienced American workforce, many of whom were women brought into the work force for the first time.

Deming was sent to Japan in 1946 by the War Department to study agricultural production and related problems in the war-damaged country (American Society for Quality 2000). Over the next two years, he made contact with Japanese statisticians and developed a lasting admiration and fondness for the Japanese people. Deming convinced Kenichi Koyanagi, one of the founding members of the Union of

Japanese Scientists and Engineers (JUSE), that statistical quality control methods could help rebuild Japanese industry.

Deming taught his first course on quality control in 1950. Over the next two decades, he would not only teach statistical methods to engineers but he would also counsel senior managers (Walton 1990). He gave his Japanese students not only statistical theory but also confidence. "I told [Japanese industrialists] Japanese quality could be the best in the world, instead of the worst," he said. Still, many were skeptical. "I was the only man in Japan who believed that Japanese industry could do that." Deming made his prophetic statement that the Japanese could capture the world market within five years if they followed his advice. "They beat my prediction. I had said it would need five years. It took four." (American Society for Quality 2000).

Meanwhile, quality control techniques were quickly discarded in the United States as American industry rushed to meet the demands of a public hungry for a wide variety of products rationed during the war years. "Quantity" not quality became the watchword. Demand for American products extended beyond our borders as most of our major competitors had their industries severely damaged as a result of the war.

It was not until 1980 when NBC aired its documentary, "If Japan Can, Why Can't We?" in which Dr. Deming was featured prominently, that American industrial leaders began to explore the quality phenomena that had transformed Japan's industry. American automobile manufacturers were among the hardest hit by Japanese competitors and they were some of Deming's first clients.

Deming's philosophy extended well beyond simply statistical control methods. "Statistical theory has changed practice in almost everything. Statistical techniques, in their ability to aid the discovery of causes, are creating a science of management and a science of administration," he said in accepting the American Society for Quality's Shewhart Medal for 1955 (American Society for Quality 2000). Deming's model developed by an American and first perfected in Japan, was a participatory form of management that drew on every employee's knowledge and abilities, at all levels, through teams and teamwork and always focused on the customer (Walton 1990). This statistician developed a system for management that has arguably met his goal of the "…transformation of the style of American management," within his lifetime (Deming 1982, ix).

Deming was a keen observer of people and one who practiced "continual improvement." "May I not learn?" he would frequently say. Certainly his management philosophy evolved over his lifetime but I believe he was influenced early in his career by his close ties with Walter Shewhart, Western Electric, and the Bell Labs.

The Hawthorne Effect

The Hawthorne Studies were conducted from 1927 to 1932 at the Western Electric Hawthorne Works in Chicago. The studies grew out of preliminary experiments at the plant from 1924 to 1927 on the effect of lighting on productivity. Those experiments showed no clear connection between productivity and the amount of illumination but researchers began to wonder what kind of changes would influence output (Elton Mayo's Hawthorne Experiments 2000). Elton Mayo, a Harvard Business School professor and management consultant, led a team of researchers to formally study the relationship between productivity and work conditions (Parson 1974). As lighting levels were increased with the test group, productivity increased. But when lighting levels were decreased, productivity continued to increase! Equally puzzling was the fact that the control group's productivity also increased even though its lighting conditions did not change. To his amazement, Mayo discovered that production increased regardless of any of the changes he made. His conclusions dealing with the positive effects of compassionate supervision and treating workers as a part of a team became known as the Hawthorne Effect (Elton Mayo's Hawthorne Experiments 2000). Thus was born the human relations school of management.

The Hawthorne studies represent the transition from the Frederick Winslow Taylor school of scientific management to the early human relations movement. This reawakened management to the understanding that their employees were capable of thinking, require intrinsic motivation, and make important decisions concerning productivity. People were much more than just robots wrapped in skin and bones that checked their brains at the entrance of the plant only to pick them up again when they left.

The Hawthorne Studies were being conducted at the very plant where Deming worked during his graduate school summers and he must have had considerable knowledge of the study and its conclusions. He told one author that some of his ideas about management were rooted in his experience at Hawthorne, where workers were paid by piecework and docked if it failed inspection (Walton 1986). Although he has not written about the full impact that the Hawthorne Effect had upon his thinking, these conclusions must have had a profound effect upon him and his evolving management theory. In Deming's 14 Points and his Theory of Profound Knowledge, we see the concepts of intrinsic motivation through meaningful work, caring, interested leadership, teamwork and participation by all the people in decision making. Many of these concepts may be traced to the Hawthorne studies.

14 Points for Management

Quality management is not a "program" to be tried and discarded when it does not meet expectations within the first quarter. Rather it is a system, a *philosophy*, a new way of looking at people and the production of goods and services. Deming never used the term "total quality management." He referred to his philosophy as "profound knowledge." This profound knowledge consisted of four interrelated parts:

1. Appreciation of a system
2. Knowledge about variation
3. The theory of knowledge, and
4. Psychology (Deming 2000).

A system, according to Deming, "...is a network of interdependent components that work together to try to accomplish the aim of the system" (Deming 2000, 95). His familiar diagram of production viewed as a system (see Figure 4-1) illustrates how each component (function, branch, division) of an organization effects every other part of the organization. A change in design, based on consumer research, may cause a change in materials and equipment. These, in turn, may cause a change in production processes, assembly procedures, or inspection cycles. Feedback from consumers, tests of processes and methods, may dictate a change in distribution procedures. Further research may call for a redesign of products that again dictates changes to material, processes, etc.

Knowledge about variation means that leaders understand that there will always be variation between people and products (Deming 2000). Just as all repeatable processes result in variation of output, whether in goods or service, likewise, people performing the same task will have different outputs.

There are a variety of causes for this variation and leaders must understand that most of the differences will be due to common causes (i.e., the variables in the process) provided the process is stable. Not understanding variation may lead to two common mistakes (Deming 2000, 99):

Figure 4-1 Production Viewed as a System

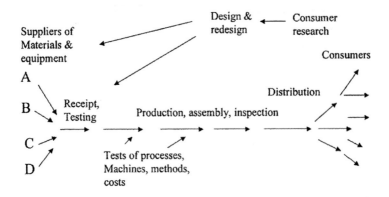

Source: Adapted from W. Edwards Deming, *Out of the Crisis*, (Cambridge, MA: MIT Center for Advanced Engineering Study, 1986), p. 4. Reprinted with permission.

1. To react to an outcome as if it came from a special cause, when actually it came from common causes of variation.
2. To treat an outcome as if it came from common causes of variation, when actually it came from a special cause.

The first mistake may be illustrated by a manager who mistakes a monthly decrease in sales (due to common causes) for a special cause and reassigns the salesman. The second mistake may be seen in the manager who does not recognize a decreased clarity in printed products due to the poor quality ink supplied by a new vendor. The problem is a special cause (poor quality ink) and not common cause variation. Either mistake could be costly.

The theory of knowledge is all about how people learn. Deming argues that without a theory, there is no learning (Deming 1982). Management in any form involves prediction (Deming 2000) and this begins with a theory of why some action has occurred. Deming's Plan, Do, Check, Act Cycle (discussed in the next chapter) begins with a theory (hypothesis) of why an event has occurred; a plan is developed to correct the problem and a small scale test is undertaken; data is collected and analyzed; and, finally action is taken on what has been learned. This leads to another hypothesis as to why our planned action did not result in the desired outcome or, if we were successful, the new process is standardized and distributed to all concerned.

Understanding psychology may be traced to Deming's Hawthorne days. People are different and they learn in different ways and at different speeds (Deming 2000). They are motivated differently. Some react favorably, in certain circumstances, to extrinsic motivators (money, titles, nice office), while others are best motivated by intrinsic factors (pride in ones work, feeling of accomplishment). Managers need to know how to motivate people to produce high quality products efficiently.

Deming's 14 Points for Management apply to organizations at all levels, large and small, in manufacturing as well as the service industry. (See Figure 4-2)

Figure 4-2

Deming's 14 Points for Management
1. **Create constancy of purpose toward improvement of product and serv**ice. This requires creation of a vision for the organization: forward-looking, creative, and innovative.
2. **Adopt the new philosophy**. This is not a program it is a philosophy that requires a long-term commitment and a new way of thinking about management and operations.
3. **Cease dependence on mass inspection**. Understand and improve the process and you will produce quality products without having to rely on inspection to assure quality. Inspection alone cannot produce quality products.
4. **End of the practice of awarding business on the basis of price tag alone**. Life-cycle costs should be considered over the lowest bidder. Work with your suppliers to help them improve their quality systems.
5. **Improve constantly and forever the system of production and service**. Quality is a never-ending journey. You never arrive at the point where you are satisfied with the quality of products.
6. **Institute training**. Train people at all levels, including management, so they can do their jobs with excellence. Understand variation and how to control it and ultimately reduce it in goods and service.
7. **Adopt and institute leadership**. Managers must become leaders who know their processes and systems and how to intrinsically motivate people.
8. **Drive out fear**. Remove fear from the workplace, both from managers and employees. When problems arise, look first to the process that management owns, and then to the person who works in the process.

Encourage people to learn.

9. **Break down barriers between staff areas**. People should work together on the development and delivery of goods and service. Develop internal customer-supplier relationships.

10. **Eliminate slogans, exhortations, and targets for the work force**. Slogans will not improve quality; understanding processes and systems will. This is the responsibility of management.

11a. **Eliminate numerical quotas for the work force**. Quotas will not improve quality; in fact, they will probably lead to poorer quality. Increased quality is only possible through process improvement.

11b. **Eliminate numerical goals for people in management**. Goals will not produce stable systems. Once systems are stable, there is no use to specify a goal. You will get whatever the system will deliver.

12. **Remove barriers that rob people of pride of workmanship**. Employees must have ownership of their processes.

13. **Encourage education and self-improvement for everyone**. Develop a "learning organization" from the bottom-up.

14. **Take action to accomplish the transformation**. Senior management must lead the new philosophy by example. People must be trained and systems created to instill a long-term commitment to quality management (Deming 1982).

5

Applying Quality Leadership

*"The single most important requirement to halt the decline
of Western industry and for America to regain worldwide
industrial competitive advantage is to fundamentally
transform the Western style of management."*
—W. Edwards Deming

Total Quality Defined

Many writers have suggested a definition for quality management. My definition considers the essence of the philosophy, its aim, methods, and intended outcome. Total quality management may be defined as: *a philosophy that empowers people to make continuous improvement, based on facts and as defined by the customer, to products through the study of processes and systems. It requires leadership.*

Let's examine the seven parts of this definition:

1. *Total quality management is a philosophy.* It is a new way of thinking about leading people in the production of goods and services. It is not a program of the month to be replaced when something better comes along.

2. *That empowers people.* The people (managers and employees) take ownership of processes and systems. They assume responsibility for continuous improvement. Management's job is to insure that the people have the tools (education, training, material, equipment) they need to do things right.

3. *To make continuous improvement.* We never accept the status quo. We are never satisfied with where we are today. We are always looking for a better way to satisfy our customers with superior goods and services.

4. *Based on facts.* We don't operate on hunches and guesses. We use data to make decisions. This begins with defining our processes and systems and measuring our current capability.

5. *As defined by the customer.* Our customers, both internal and external, provide feedback to us on our products. If they are not satisfied, we are not satisfied. The customer ultimately decides if we are successful.

6. *To products through the study of processes and systems.* We understand our processes and systems and what they are capable of producing. We continually look for ways to improve these processes to

reduce variation and improve quality and to develop new processes, where required.

7. *It requires leadership.* All this does not happen by chance. If top leadership is not driving the philosophy it will eventually fail. This requires a continuous drumbeat of support and leadership by example.

Principles of Total Quality

Quality management is characterized by four principles:

- *Strong customer focus.* Our customers define our success and we will develop processes and systems to insure that the voice of the customer is heard throughout the development and deployment of our products.

- *Definition and deployment to all employees of objectives and values that ensure success.* We will involve all of our people in the definition and deployment of our strategic and tactical objectives and goals. We will also clearly define our guiding principles and insure that everyone in the organization both understands and is committed to their fulfillment.

- *Enablement and empowerment of all employees.* We see our employees as valued assets not liabilities to be used and abused. Accordingly, we will provide continuous education and training for all employees and push decision making to the lowest possible level through process ownership.

- *Definition, control, and improvement of all key business processes.* We will identify and define our key business processes and bring them under statistical control. We will then work to reduce variation and to continuously improve these processes and systems so that we produce superior products that meet or exceed our customer's expectations.

Process Improvement

Dr. Deming introduced to the Japanese in 1950 a method for process improvement, referred to as the Deming cycle, the PDCA cycle, or as Deming called it, the Shewhart cycle (Deming 1982). Figure 5-1 illustrates the cycle.

Figure 5-1 The Shewhart Cycle

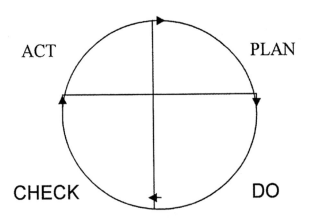

Source: Adapted from W. Edwards Deming, *Out of the Crisis*, (Cambridge, MA: MIT Center for Advanced Engineering Study, 1986), p. 88. Reprinted with permission.

The cycle begins with *planning*. What are we going to study? What do we want to improve? What are the key parameters that should be observed? How shall we collect data? Once these questions are answered, a team will plan a change or test. The *do* phase is where we carry out the change or test, preferably on a small scale. The *check*, or *study* phase, is where we observe the effects of the change or test. We collect data. Finally, the *act* phase is where we take action on what we have learned from our small-scale test. Did we achieve our goals? If we did, then why did we? If we did not, then why not? Once we are satisfied with the revision to our process, our changes are incorporated into the process procedures and disseminated to all hands.

The Deming cycle must have resonated with the Japanese spirit as they could immediately see a similarity between it and the Asian philosophical understanding of the circle of life, the ying and yang. This Christian from the West, whose hobby was composing liturgical music for the organ, was speaking the language of the orient.

Quality Leadership Functions

Dr. Curt Reimann, former Director of the Malcolm Baldrige National Quality Award, benchmarked Baldrige award winners over several years and found the following common leadership characteristics:
- Leaders were visible, committed, and knowledgeable.
- They displayed a missionary zeal for quality.
- They set aggressive targets.
- They had strong drivers that kept their systems on track.
- They effectively communicated their values.
- They were well organized.
- They maintained personal customer contact.

These characteristics are consistent with the behaviors or *functions* of a leader as described by Dr. Deming:

- *They understand how their group's work fits into the vision of the organization.* They can conceptualize and explain to their followers the importance of the work they perform.

- *They focus on customers, both internal and external.* In most processes, more than one person performs some work on the product (goods or service). This sets up a customer-supplier relationship within the process. The customer asks, "Here's what I want from you." And the supplier responds, "Here's what I can do for you." By finding out the customer's requirements, the internal supplier can better meet the needs of that customer. Likewise, the external customer is that business or consumer who receives our product. What are the needs of that customer and are we meeting them?
- *They are coaches not judges.* Coaches are on the field with the team members sharing their emotions, encouraging, disciplining, and cheering them on. Judges sit up in the stands and critique from afar. Coaches lead from the front.
- *They remove obstacles to joy in work.* Leaders discover whatever is causing discouragement in the workplace, whether it's shoddy material, poor equipment, unhealthy working conditions, or lack of training. They provide what people need to succeed and find fulfillment in their work.
- *They learn who is in need of special help.* Most people will perform their work within the range of common cause variation when compared to others performing the same work. Some few people need special help. It is the leader's job to identify those needing special help and to provide them whatever is needed. Sometimes this will mean moving them to another job more suited to their skills and abilities.
- *They work to constantly improve their process or system.* Leaders set the example in continually work-

ing to improve their own processes as well as those processes and systems which they manage.

- *They create trust.* Before a leader can create a culture of trust among his followers he must first demonstrate that he is *trustworthy*. This means that leaders are true to their word, will maintain a confidence, and will always tell the truth even when it hurts.
- *They forgive mistakes.* Leaders recognize that most problems are caused by process errors for which the follower usually has no control; e.g., a bad lot of material or out of tolerance machinery. Those few times when human error is responsible for problems (Deming says that's only about 15% of the time, hence the 85/15 rule), leaders forgive and forget.
- *They listen!* Leaders are active listeners who encourage their followers to talk about ways to improve processes and systems. They recognize that often those who work *in* the process (hourly employees) have a much better idea of what needs to be done to improve than do those who work *on* the process (managers) (Deming 1988).

Figure 5-2 contrasts traditional leadership behaviors with quality leadership.

Figure 5-2

Traditional vs. Quality Leadership

Traditional Leaders	Quality Leaders
◆ Bossing	◆ Coaching
◆ Extrinsic motivation	◆ Intrinsic motivation
◆ Authoritative	
◆ Control	◆ Participative
◆ Reactive followers	◆ Empowerment
◆ Selected communication	◆ Proactive followers
◆ Short-term planning	◆ Open communication
◆ Centralized decision-making	◆ Long-term planning
◆ Bureaucracy	◆ Decentralized decision-making
◆ Structure	◆ Teams
◆ Individual rewards	◆ Process
◆ Competition	◆ Group rewards
	◆ Cooperation

Adapted from Hughes, Ginnett, Curphy (1993)

Creating a Quality Culture

Peter Senge, in *The Leader's New Work* (1990), defined a three-fold role for leaders in creating a quality culture. The leader must be a:
- Designer
- Steward
- Teacher

The *designer* role involves leading the effort to define

guiding principles for the organization; i.e., *vision, mission, and values*. The leader should not develop these alone but she must create the environment that produces these principles. The leader's role is to facilitate and encourage consensus on what the organization does now (mission), where it wants to go (vision), and what it stands for (values). Often this involves the senior executives developing a draft set of guiding principles and then distributing them for critique and debate throughout the organization. Stephen Covey suggests attaching the tag, "We don't like them either!" with the draft version to encourage critical debate.

The *steward* role means empowering others to take necessary actions to achieve the aims of the organization. There are a very few tasks that the senior leader alone must do—all others should be delegated. This means that along with *responsibility* must go *authority* and *accountability*. Leaders cannot hold people responsible for a task without also giving them authority to expend resources and then hold them accountable for their results. Decision-making should be pushed to the lowest level possible especially with customer contact associates. Let me illustrate with a story.

A group from our church planned to attend a conference of evangelical Christians in Boston. We all made our reservations at a hotel across the street from the convention center because the hotel told us that parking (always a premium in Boston) was included in the price of the room. My wife and I drove up with our good friends. At the hotel, we dropped off the ladies at the front desk while the husbands parked the car in the adjacent parking garage. When we struggled inside with the luggage, my wife told me that the hotel had given them each a voucher for brunch. We all agreed that was a nice touch!

Check out time was noon the next day but since our conference continued until 4:00 p.m., we checked out early during a break and stored our luggage. When I got to the desk and received my bill, I asked if I was to receive a stamp for parking? The clerk looked dumbfounded and proceeded to tell me that parking was paid for separately by the customer directly to the garage. After a fruitless conversation with the desk clerk, I asked to see the manager. He arrived promptly and I told him that we had specifically chosen to stay at his hotel because of the free parking. I told him that I was a very unhappy customer to learn that was not the case. He finally enlightened me to their policy of providing free parking or a brunch voucher—but not both.

"And I see here that you had two brunches this morning," he said with a little smirk!

"But no one told us it was parking or brunch!" I replied. I left a frustrated customer, paid the garage fee and drove home steaming.

At about the same time, a female marketing executive was attending another convention in Boston and she too checked out of her hotel early. Presented with her bill, she demanded to know why she was being charged with two Sunday brunches at $25 each when she had not eaten at the hotel! The desk clerk apologized and disappeared with her bill to the back office. She returned in a few minutes with a new bill minus the offending charge. The executive paid her bill and returned to her convention.

An hour into the next meeting, it dawned on her that she had, in fact, eaten at the hotel. At the next break, she rushed back to the hotel relieved to find the same desk clerk on duty. Stepping to the counter, she profusely apologized for her rude behavior earlier and stated that she just remembered that she had, in fact, gone to brunch and had taken a client. Would the clerk please add that to her bill? The young clerk looked at the woman and said, "Ma'am, there is no need to correct your bill."

"But," the woman said, " did you know that I'd eaten brunch?"

"Yes," the clerk replied, "I went back and checked your signature on the charge."

"Then why didn't you tell me that and leave it on my bill?"

"Ma'am, I could see that you were very upset and your good will is worth more to the Ritz Carlton than $50!"

This is empowerment. Both clerks knew what needed to be done to satisfy the customer but only one was empowered to take action. In fact, at the first hotel, even the duty manager was not empowered to do what he knew was right to satisfy the customer. (Adapted from a speech by Stephen Covey (1993) and the author's own experience.)

Before empowering people, leaders must first *enable* them with education, training, equipment, and the financial resources needed to accomplish their responsibilities.

Leaders must then create policies and implement programs to establish the new approach to decision-making.

Finally, the *teacher* role involves modeling behavior supportive of the new culture. People will listen to what you are saying but they will be convinced of your sincerity only when they see you act according to those new values. If you say that one of your values is that you will never lie to a customer but when faced with an important order that you know will be late, you fudge a little on the delivery date or blame it on your shipper, you will have lost your credibility and your values are meaningless. The more senior leaders become, the more teaching they should do. Unfortunately, many senior executives are too busy to teach and their organizations suffer as a result when they retire.

> *"Setting an example is not the main means of influencing another...it is the only means."*
> —*Albert Einstein*

In this chapter, we have examined total quality management and its contribution to leadership theory. I believe that Deming's management system has transformed the style of American management and the flat, team-based organizational structures that we see in business today are largely a result of his leadership approach. I also believe that this leadership approach is very compatible with servant leadership—one complements the other. With that in mind, we turn now to Robert Greenleaf and his understanding of the concept of servant as leader.

6

Greenleaf's Servant Leadership

Good leaders must first become good servants.
—Robert K. Greenleaf

Although the concept of servant as leader has been around for at least 2000 years, the most recognized modern proponent of this leadership philosophy was Robert K. Greenleaf (1904-1990). Greenleaf spent his first career in management research, development and education at AT&T (Robert K. Greenleaf Center for Servant Leadership 1996). After retirement, he began a second career teaching and consulting and founded The Center for Applied Ethics. Today it is known as the Robert K. Greenleaf Center, located in Indianapolis, Indiana. Although Greenleaf does not refer directly to Jesus' teaching as instrumental in development of his understanding of leadership, his Quaker faith is evident throughout his writings.

Background

Greenleaf writes that the servant leader concept emerged after his involvement with leaders and directors on college campuses during the tumultuous 1960's and early 1970's (Greenleaf 1977). He attributes his understanding of servant as leader to Hermann Hesse's *The Journey to the East* (Hesse 1956). This is the story of a band of men on a mythical journey. The central figure is Leo, an able servant and their guide. All goes well on the journey as long as Leo is around to direct, organize, and provide for the needs of the travelers. Suddenly one morning the travelers wake to find Leo is gone. The group quickly falls apart and shortly thereafter disbands as each man returns home dejected and disappointed. The narrator begins a search for Leo and after many years finds him. The group that had sponsored the fateful trip takes the narrator into its Order where he discovers that Leo is its head, its guiding spirit, and a great and noble leader.

Greenleaf understood the message of Hesse's story was that the great leader is seen as servant first (Greenleaf 1977). Leo was the leader all along but he was first a servant because that's what he was at his core. Leadership was bestowed on Leo but he remained a servant in his heart. Evangelist Billy Graham relates a similar real-life story in his autobiography, *Just As I Am* (1997).

> Mr. Graham and five other men flew from Calcutta to Dimapur, Nepal where they boarded trucks for their final leg to Kohima, 7,000 feet above sea level. When they arrived, the soccer stadium where Mr. Graham was scheduled to preach already had 90,000 people inside with many thousands more outside several hours before the meetings

were to begin. The schedule included an early morning service and Bible-study prior to the main meeting at which Mr. Graham would preach. When he asked about how many were expected for the early service and Bible-study, he was told, "About 100,000 people." Of course, Mr. Graham decided to lead the service and Bible study himself rather than have a staff member lead. As the party was shown to their quarters in the government house, they were introduced to a man named Nihuli, who would handle their baggage, make tea, and do whatever else needed doing. As Nihuli was cleaning their shoes, Mr. Graham asked him who would be leading the early-morning service just before the Bible teaching that he would lead. At first Nihuli didn't reply, but when pressed he admitted that he would be teaching the Bible to the huge crowd. Graham confessed that, "The man cleaning my shoes had just taught me a lesson on the servant attitude and spirit of ministering so often adopted by Christ Himself." (Graham 1997, 279)

Similarly, several years ago I was told the story of a famous Japanese evangelist who slipped off to the men's room prior to his turn to speak to a large crowd. After several minutes, his associates became concerned as the man had not returned and his time to speak was rapidly approaching. Walking into the restroom, his associates found the evangelist on his knees under the counter picking up paper towels that had been discarded around the overflowing trashcan. Incredulous, the men asked what was he doing? He replied, "How can we speak of the love of Jesus to all men while we abuse the dignity of the least of these by our slovenliness?" Both of these stories relate to the traits and characteristics of a servant leader as taught by Jesus Christ but are similar to Hesse's Leo.

> *"If a good society is to be built, one that is more just and more caring, and where the less able and more able serve one another with unlimited liability, then the best way is to raise the performance as servant of institutions, and sanction natural servants to serve and lead."*
> —*Robert K. Greenleaf*

Greenleaf defines a servant leader as one who begins first with the desire to serve and then makes the conscious choice to aspire to lead (Greenleaf 1977). This is a sharply different definition from one who aspires to a position of leadership due to a need for power, position, or wealth. The servant-first attitude insures that the priority needs of others are being served.

Servant Leader traits

The *traits* of a servant leader include *initiative, intelligence, foresight*, and *perception*. Let's briefly examine each of these.

> *"To venture causes anxiety, but not to venture is to lose one's self. And to venture in the highest sense is precisely to become conscious of one's self."*
> —Soren Kierkegaard

Initiative. Someone must take the initiative, provide the ideas, and add the structure. This is the leader's job. He must also assume the risk of failure along with the opportunity for success.

Intelligence. Greenleaf argues that the leader must have a sense of the *unknowable* and be able to foresee the *unforeseeable* (Greenleaf 1977). Since decision-making always involves some degree of uncertainty, leaders need to be able to apply *intuition* to their decision process. Early studies of leader's traits concluded that intelligence was a dominate trait for leaders; however, this trait was not a valid predictor of leaders (Stogdill 1948, Mann 1959). At least one more recent study has concurred that intelligence *was* a valid trait for leaders (Lord, DeVader, and Allinger 1986).

Foresight. Leaders have the ability to conceptualize the present along with the past and the future and to articulate to followers how it all fits together. Greenleaf argues this requires faith at the conscious level that ones' experience and knowledge will provide intuitive insight and result in superior performance (Greenleaf 1977).

Perception. Leaders always have their antennas up and have a wide span of awareness. Greenleaf says leaders are "sharply awake and reasonably disturbed" (Greenleaf, 1977, 28). By that he means that leaders are not satisfied with the status quo. They are constantly looking for ways to improve. Leaders are more perceptive of the environment than others and what needs to be done to succeed. Leaders need to cloak themselves with "an armor of confidence" (Greenleaf 1977, 28) in facing the unknown (see Paul's instructions to "Put on the whole armor of God..." (Ephesians 6:11)). Superior perception and self-confidence allow leaders to make decisions under conditions of uncertainty and risk.

Servant Leader behaviors

The *behaviors* of servant leaders include *trust, listening and understanding, acceptance and empathy,* and *use of power.* Again, I will briefly describe the ways in which servant leaders interact with their followers.

> *"Legitimacy begins with trust."*
> —*Robert K. Greenleaf*

Trust. A servant leader builds trust among his followers. He does this first by being *trustworthy.* He is true to his word. He is not afraid to admit that he does not have all the answers and he is quick to apologize when he has wronged someone. He can maintain a confidence. He does not hold back bad news. He looks out for the welfare of his employees. Men and women have confidence in leaders they respect and trust, knowing that the leader will always have their well being in mind under all conditions (Puryear, 1971).

This is often a challenge to a young college graduate who is hired in a leadership position by virtue of his education alone. This person is placed over men and women who are often older and certainly much more experienced than their new supervisor. That young supervisor's attitude toward his employees will determine whether he builds trust among them and is successful or is left to fail on his own.

Obviously, he needs the cooperation and wisdom that his employees bring to the job. He can achieve that by being trustworthy. By being straightforward and honest with his employees about his lack of experience and his faith in their knowledge and experience, he will begin to bridge the gulf of suspicion between them and him.

> *"To lead is to serve, if for no other reason than that every leader should conduct himself as though his work, no matter how secular, is in the service of God. Moreover, as in the Gospels, the rule of leadership is that to whom much is given, much is expected, and a leader must do what he can for those less well placed than himself."*
> —*H. W. Crocker III*, Robert E. Lee, On Leadership

Listening and understanding. One of Stephen Covey's *Seven Habits* (1989, 235) is to "seek first to understand than to be understood." A natural servant responds by listening first. He practices active listening. General Dwight David Eisenhower, then Supreme Allied Commander during World War II, had this characteristic, "... he looked you straight in the eye and listened very intently to everything that you had to say. To my mind it was this quality of appearing to be completely absorbed in what one was saying that formed the basis of Ike's engaging personality" (Puryear, 1971, 19). Often, this means that a leader will ask questions to insure that he thoroughly understands the other's position before responding. Most of the time, in personal and professional settings, we are too busy crafting our brilliant response to the other person's complaints to actually hear what they are saying. An active listener hears and understands the other person's position before responding. Summarizing the other's position will help to clarify the issue for the leader: "I understand that you are saying that you believe you were not selected for the supervisor's position because you are a woman? Is that right?" When this technique is practiced, leaders often find that the problem is easily resolved or disappears with new understanding from both parties.

A leader must communicate in a language and context that is meaningful to her listeners. Jesus used this technique often in his parables. He would illustrate a principle by using the everyday experiences of his listeners; e.g., the sower and the seed (Mark 4:3-9), the wheat and the tares (Matthew 13:24-30), the mustard seed (Matthew 13:31, 32), the hidden treasure (Matthew 13:44), and the valuable pearl (Matthew 13:45, 46). When Jesus taught, sixty-five percent of the time he used stories drawn from his personal experience, history, the Old Testament, and his imagination (Wilkinson 1994).

A leader must communicate at the listener's level of understanding. Speaking down to followers is as bad as speaking over their heads. Selected use of esoteric language, i.e., terms and acronyms known exclusively to a profession, trade, or craft, demonstrates respect and trust and can forge an "insider's" relationship between leader and followers.

Acceptance and empathy. The servant leader always accepts people as they are and empathizes with them. He never rejects people but he does reject substandard effort. Accepting people means that leaders are tolerant of mistakes and less-than-perfect performance. Often we learn best from our mistakes. The servant leader will tolerate mistakes and even encourage them.

I used to enjoy watching the faces of new officers in my command when I would tell them that I *expected* them to make mistakes! I could almost hear them thinking, is this guy nuts? I would go on to explain to them that if they were not making mistakes, they were not trying anything new. How were they going to make improvements without trying new ways of doing things? "Don't be satisfied with the status quo," I'd say. "Experiment, try out new procedures, just don't stay too long with a failing project."

The servant leader strives for synergy. He aims to lift a team of people to grow beyond what they otherwise would have thought possible.

> *"A great man is always willing to be little."*
> —*Ralph Waldo Emerson*

Power and authority. Servant leaders use the power of persuasion and example, not coercion, to lead others and to create opportunities to build their own autonomy. This is true even in military organizations where obedience is assumed, as reflected in General Eisenhower's thesis that,

> ... in all commands the high commander's success "will be measured more by his ability to lead and persuade than by his adherence to fixed notions of arbitrary command practices" (Puryear 1971, 217).

However, Greenleaf recognized that in this fallen world, authority backed up by power is sometimes still necessary (Greenleaf 1977). His practical definition of management reflects his pragmatism: "management is the study of how things get done" (Robert K. Greenleaf Center for Servant Leadership 1996). He argued that servant leaders are functionally superior at seeing, hearing, knowing, and with intuitive insight.

> *"Leadership by persuasion has the virtue of change by convincement rather than coercion. Its advantages are obvious."*
> —*Robert K. Greenleaf*

The account of Joseph, as recorded in the Book of Genesis, illustrates this type of leader.

Joseph, the eleventh of twelve sons of Jacob and obviously a favorite of his father's, was sold into slavery at the age of 17 by his jealous brothers. Stolen from his home and his family, Joseph was eventually transported to Egypt and sold to one of Pharaoh's officials, Potiphar, the captain of the guard. Joseph quickly became a trusted and efficient servant and Potiphar soon put him in charge of his entire household and everything that he owned. "So he left in Joseph's care everything he had; with Joseph in charge, he did not concern himself with anything except the food he ate." (Genesis 39:6) Just when things were looking up for Joseph, the second major calamity in his life struck. Potiphar's wife tried to seduce him and when he refused she cried rape! Joseph's angry master had him thrown into prison.

Joseph's godly character and abilities soon came to the attention of the jailer. "(T)he LORD was with him; he showed him kindness and granted him favor in the eyes of the prison warden. So the warden put Joseph in charge of all those held in the prison, and he was made responsible for all that was done there. The warden paid no attention to anything under Joseph's care, because the LORD was with Joseph and gave him success in whatever he did" (Genesis 39:21-23). Here is Joseph again as a servant, or in this case as a prisoner, and again he is elevated to a position of leadership by others who recognize his innate ability to lead.

Some time later, Pharaoh's chief cupbearer and baker were implicated in a conspiracy against the king and thrown into the same prison with Joseph. When Joseph came to them the next morning, he found them dejected. The men related that they had both had bad dreams and did not know what they meant. Joseph correctly interpreted the dreams and his prophecy was fulfilled three days later. As Joseph had foretold, the cupbearer was restored to his position but the chief baker was hanged. Meanwhile, Joseph continued to languish in prison.

Two years later, Pharaoh had a dream that all the magicians and wise men of Egypt could not interpret. Suddenly the chief cupbearer remembered Joseph who was summoned to Pharaoh's court. "'I had a dream, and no one can interpret it,' Pharaoh said. 'But I have heard it said of you that when you hear a dream you can interpret it.' 'I cannot do it,' Joseph replied to Pharaoh, 'but God will give Pharaoh the answer he desires'" (Genesis 40:15,16). After hearing his dream, Joseph told Pharaoh that God was showing him that there would be a severe famine in the land following seven years of plenty. He went on to recommend a course of action to prepare for the coming disaster. Pharaoh was so impressed with Joseph's godly wisdom that he immediately placed him in charge of "...the whole land of Egypt" (Genesis 41:41).

Joseph did prepare Egypt for the famine that was to come as he had prophesied and was eventfully reunited with his family. He was an archetype of a servant leader; a man who was a servant first and then due to his godly character-istics and innate abilities was elevated to a position of lead-ership. Thirteen centuries later, another young man in similar circumstances was called to a position of leadership due to his strength of character and abilities. Most know of him due to his miraculous rescue from the den of lions, but he was also a servant first.

Daniel was among the "...sons of Israel, including some of the royal family and of the nobles..." who were carried off to Babylon by Nebuchadnezzar in 606 B.C. (Daniel 1:3) He was identified as one of the young men "...in whom was no defect, who were good-looking, showing intelligence in every branch of wisdom ...and who had ability for serving in the king's court." (Daniel 1:4). He quickly distinguished himself in the foreign king's court as "God gave (him) knowledge and intelligence in every branch of literature and wisdom; Daniel even understood all kinds of visions and dreams." (Daniel 1:17)

This was soon put to the test when Nebuchadnezzar had a troubling dream and no one could interpret the meaning of the dream. When the king issued a decree to kill all the wise men of Babylon, Daniel went to him and requested time to discern the interpretation of the dream. The king agreed and Daniel and his friends prayed that the LORD would reveal its meaning and thereby save them and the other wise men.

God did reveal the meaning of Nebuchadnezzar's dream to Daniel and when he interpreted it for the king Daniel was elevated to "...ruler over the whole province of Babylon and chief prefect over all the wise men of Babylon." (Daniel 2:48)

Years later, when Daniel was an old man, he again was appointed to high position by Darius, king of the Medes. Named one of three ruling commissioners with responsibility over the whole kingdom, "...this Daniel began distinguishing himself among the commissioners and satraps because he possessed an extraordinary spirit, and the king planned to appoint him over the entire kingdom." (Daniel 6:3)

Like Joseph before him, Daniel was taken captive from his home and family as a young man and raised in a foreign culture as a servant. He was elevated to leadership not

by his own design but by his godly characteristics and innate abilities.

In the next chapter we'll examine the impact that leaders
like Joseph and Daniel could have upon our businesses and
our culture.

7

Greenleaf's Servant Leadership Applied

"The best test, though difficult to administer, is: Do those
served grow as persons; do they while being served,
become healthier, wiser, free, more autonomous, more likely
themselves to become servants?"
—Robert K. Greenleaf

Implications for Society

What are the implications for society where servant leadership is emulated and respected? In such a society, able servants with the potential to lead will lead. Where appropriate, they will follow only other servant leaders. Preparation on the part of those servants who would be leaders must be the first priority. A servant leader prepares by serving, by studying, and by doing.

The pragmatist in Greenleaf warns that servant leaders

must be realistic since people will choose order over chaos even if they have to give up much of their freedom (Greenleaf 1977). These words, written during the height of the Cold War, have proven prophetic in some of the republics of the former Soviet Union, as ex-Communist rulers, lightly disguised as reformers, have returned to power in the name of order.

This human propensity to seek order over freedom has been true at least since the time of the Exodus of the children of Israel from Egypt when God set the Israelites free from the oppressive hand of pharaoh. Only forty-five days after being miraculously released from bondage, the people began to complain against their leaders. "Then the whole congregation of the children of Israel complained against Moses and Aaron in the wilderness. And the children of Israel said to them,

> 'Oh, that we had died by the hand of the LORD in the land of Egypt, when we sat by the pots of meat and when we ate bread to the full! For you have brought us out into this wilderness to kill this whole assembly with hunger.'" (Exodus 16:2, 3)

Summary

To sum up the distinguishing qualities of a servant leader:

- *Accepts unlimited liability for others.* The leader allows followers the freedom to make mistakes while accepting them as them are. He deflects praise to subordinates and accepts criticism from superiors for mistakes made by followers under his authority.
- *Knows self well.* A servant leader is confident in his

abilities and strengths. He recognizes his own weaknesses and works to improve them. He has the confidence to allow others to make decisions and even to make mistakes.

* *Holder of a liberating vision.* Servant leaders are visionaries who are able to see beyond the here and now into the future and are able to lead others toward that vision.

* *User of persuasion.* Servant leaders strive for consensus through persuasion. They are open to the ideas of their followers and recognize that they don't have all the answers. Rather than force an issue by coercion, they will attempt to persuade their followers of the benefits of their solution. The result will be commitment to the decision on the part of the followers, not just compliance.

* *Builder of community.* The servant leader builds community by caring for her followers and encouraging them to care for others, too. She builds trust by being trustworthy. The result is an organization that holds the needs of its people equally important to the needs of the organization.

* *Uses power ethically.* The servant leader uses power to promote the good of the whole and not for self-promotion. However, he is a pragmatist who recognizes that sometimes power is needed to bring about change but he does so with the highest ethical standards.

> *Jesus said to them, "The kings of the Gentiles lord it over them; and those who exercise authority over them call themselves benefactors. But you are not to be like that. Instead, the greatest among you should be like the youngest, and the one who rules like the one who serves."*
>
> *—Luke 22:25, 26*

Institutional Leadership Traditions

Greenleaf presents two traditions for institutional leadership. The first he describes as the hierarchical tradition dating from the time of Moses. This tradition places one person in charge at the top. The second type, from Roman times, is the form where the principle leadership is *primus inter pares*—first among equals (Greenleaf 1977).

Certainly the hierarchical tradition has been around much longer than from the time of Moses. We can trace it back to at least 2,200 B.C. when Abram is called by God to leave Haran and go to the land of Canaan:

> Now the LORD had said to Abram:
> "Get out of your country, from your family and from your father's house, to a land that I will show you. I will make you a great nation; I will bless you and make your name great; and you shall be a blessing. I will bless those who bless you, and I will curse him who curses you; and in you all the families of the earth shall be blessed." (Genesis 12:1-3)

The traditional, paternal leadership form has dominated most cultures up to our modern times. However, going back even to the time of Moses the single leader/decision-maker model had problems. After God had miraculously led the Israelites out of Egypt, their first battle was with the Amalekites. The following passage is a symbolic illustration of the value of shared leadership.

> "And so it was, when Moses held up his hand, that Israel prevailed; and when he let down his hand, Amalek prevailed. But Moses' hands became heavy; so they took a stone and put it under him, and he sat on it. And Aaron and Hur supported his hands, one on one side, and the other on the other side; and his hands were steady until the going down of the sun." (Exodus 17:11, 12)

The Israelites went on to defeat the Amalekites and Moses learned an important lesson in leadership: *leaders need trusted followers to hold them up when the burden of leadership becomes too heavy.*

Not long after this encounter, Moses' father-in-law Jethro came to him in the wilderness returning his wife and two sons whom Moses had sent home during the plagues in Egypt. Moses was about to learn another valuable lesson in leadership.

> And so it was, on the next day, that Moses sat to judge the people; and the people stood before Moses from morning until evening. So when Moses' father-in-law saw all that he did for the people, he said, "What is this thing that you are doing for the people? Why do you alone sit, and all the people

stand before you from morning until evening?" And Moses said to his father-in-law, "Because the people come to me to inquire of God. When they have a difficulty, they come to me, and I judge between one and another; and I make known the statutes of God and His laws."

So Moses' father-in-law said to him, "The thing that you do is not good. Both you and these people who are with you will surely wear yourselves out. For this thing is too much for you; you are not able to perform it by yourself. Listen now to my voice; I will give you counsel, and God will be with you: Stand before God for the people, so that you may bring the difficulties to God. And you shall teach them the statutes and the laws, and show them the way in which they must walk and the work they must do. Moreover you shall select from all the people able men, such as fear God, men of truth, hating covetousness; and place such over them to be rulers of thousands, rulers of hundreds, rulers of fifties, and rulers of tens. And let them judge the people at all times. Then it will be that every great matter they shall bring to you, but every small matter they themselves shall judge. So it will be easier for you, for they will bear the burden with you." (Exodus 18:13-22)

Moses learned the value of *delegation*. In chapter 5, we examined the leadership role of *steward* and the importance of delegation of authority, responsibility and accountability. Here Moses is instructed by his father-in–law in this important principle of leadership.

In their second year of wandering in the wilderness, Moses was continually beset by the complaints of the people. Finally, he cried out to the LORD,

> "I am not able to bear all these people along, because the burden is too heavy for me. If you treat me like this, please kill me here and now—if I have found favor in Your sight—and do not let me see my wretchedness!"
>
> So the LORD said to Moses: "Gather to Me seventy men of the elders of Israel, whom you know to be the elders of the people and officers over them; bring them to the tabernacle of meeting, that they may stand there with you. Then I will come down and talk with you there. I will take of the Spirit that is upon you and will put the same upon them; and they shall bear the burden of the people with you, that you may not bear it yourself alone." (Numbers 11:14-17)

What other authority do we need than God himself who instructs Moses to share decision-making with the elders of the people? These passages illustrate that the single chief tradition has had recognized shortcomings long before the modern era. Even with a hierarchical structure, a single decision maker cannot hope to "hold his hands up alone." Following the pattern of Moses, leaders must share decision-making through delegation of authority, responsibility, and accountability while reserving only the most important decisions to themselves.

The second tradition, and the one favored by Greenleaf, is the *primus inter pares*. First among equals may have been the ideal leadership form during the Roman Empire; however, man's sinful nature often overcame good intentions and many who ruled Rome did so alone fearful of sharing power with anyone. Perhaps the closest form to *primus inter pares* was in mythological Camelot. King Arthur's Round Table depicted shared leadership among the King's senior staff. King Arthur was "first among equals" and decision-making was by consensus. This apparently is a concept difficult for Westerners to understand as illustrated in the Hollywood film, *First Knight.* One scene in the film has King Arthur (Sean Connery) inviting Lancelot (Richard Gere) into the King's conference room, which is dominated by the Round Table. The King explains to young Lancelot their unique form of leadership where the King is merely one voice at the table along with the other senior knights. Apparently, the film's director can't fathom this concept because a few minutes later we see Arthur making a unilateral decision to award Lancelot the vacant seat at the table!

Primus inter pares may be a difficult concept for Hollywood to grasp but we are seeing more leadership sharing in American business than ever before. In December 1996, the *Wall Street Journal* reported that Microsoft Corporation had created a nine-member executive committee headed by its Chairman and Chief Executive Bill Gates (Clark 1996). This new leadership team replaced a group called the Office of the President, which started in 1992 with a team of three and had expanded over the years to seven members. Apparently Mr. Gates had recognized that the single chief concept simply would not work in his rapidly expanding technology empire.

I believe that Mr. Greenleaf's preference for *primus inter pares,* as a leadership form may result, in part, from his Quaker background. Excerpts from a description of a business meeting from *Quaker Business Meetings: How Friends Make Decisions* will illustrate:

A Quaker "meeting for business" is also held in the context of worship. The aim of a meeting for business is to seek the will of God. It is not a matter of bowing to the will of the majority, as Friends do not vote. It is an exercise of listening to God through what each person says. If the Clerk is not able to discern a clear sense of the meeting, no decision will be taken, and no minute will be made except to record that the meeting is not ready to proceed (Glasgow Quaker Meeting 1995).

In the Quaker business meeting we see the principle of *primus inter pares* and decision-making by consensus. Are there other reasons for favoring shared leadership over a single decision maker? Let's examine Greenleaf's critique.

Criticism of the Single Chief

Greenleaf argues that the single chief concept is abnormal and corrupting. He would agree with Lord Acton that, "Power corrupts; absolute power corrupts absolutely." Regretfully, almost daily it seems we are reminded of leaders in all walks of life who have succumbed to the corrupting influence of unchecked power. As we enter the 21st century, cynicism abounds among the American electorate as senior government officials are exposed to have abused a position of trust to further their own political agendas. This is particularly damaging when the abuser is a respected leader in the church. One Christian leader stands head and shoulders above the rest: Billy Graham. Recognizing early in his career the corrupting influence of power, Mr. Graham established a close group of associates to hold him accountable (Graham 1997). With God's help and the encouragement of his friends, this man, one of the most respected persons in the world, has remained as humble as that lanky farm boy from Charlotte, North Carolina who left home to be an evangelist many years ago.

> *"The abuse of power is curbed if the holder of power is surrounded by equals who are strong, and if there is close oversight by a monitoring group, trustees who are not involved in the daily use of power."*
> —*Robert K. Greenleaf*

A single chief leader often develops a self-protective image of omniscience. Again, we see human nature at work. When the leader only hears fawning words of praise over every action and decision, she will naturally begin to believe that she has all the answers. This can lead to disastrous results for any organization. I worked for such a leader. He was a brilliant man who came to believe only in the counsel of one: himself. He would often humiliate his senior "advisors" by initially advocating one position in a discussion and then, when his senior aids agreed with him, take the other side while castigating them for their lack of insight! As his belief in his own omniscience grew, his effectiveness as a leader diminished. At the end of his term in office he had lost nearly all effectiveness and was immersed in corruption investigations involving his top aids.

Leaders must have staff members who are not afraid to question, to probe, to take opposing positions, to become the "devil's advocate." Without this dialectic approach, decision-making is subject to *groupthink*, defined as the deterioration of mental efficiency, reality testing, and moral judgment in the interest of group solidarity (Janis 1982). The decision-making surrounding the Cuban Missile Crisis of October 1962, the closest the world ever came to nuclear war, illustrates this concept.

President John Kennedy had received photographic intelligence that the Russians were moving intermediate-range ballistic missiles (MRBMs) in to Cuba, just 90 miles from the American mainland. Kennedy immediately assembled the EX-COMM (Executive Committee of the National Security Counsel), twelve of his most important advisors, and sought their counsel. The initial position favored by a majority of the group called for an immediate air strike on the missile sites along with an amphibious landing of American troops. Only the President's brother, Robert Kennedy, the Attorney General, openly opposed the plan. Communication was opened with the Soviets, including an important back channel between Robert Kennedy and Soviet Ambassador Dobrynin, informing their leadership that the missiles had to be removed while the President's group debated the proper course of action. After watching the situation develop and debating the best course of action over several days, the group came to a decision to establish a naval blockade (officially referred to as a "quarantine" as a blockade was an act of war) of Cuba until the Soviets removed the missiles. Both American and Soviet navies were at sea and steaming toward each other while the anxiety mounted among the leadership of the two countries. At the crucial moment, the Soviet ships turned back. Upon hearing the good news, Secretary of State Dean Rusk turned to McGeorge Bundy and said, "We've been eyeball to eyeball and the other fellow just blinked." Shortly thereafter, the Soviets began removing the missiles.

> *"I thought I might never live to see another Saturday night."*
> *—Secretary of Defense Robert McNamara*

Robert Kennedy played the role of "devil's advocate" during the long days of anxious debate over the best course of action. He was in a unique position, being the President's brother, and therefore felt free to oppose the group and suggest alternative solutions. We are fortunate that he did for we now know that the missiles were targeted on American cities and that the Soviets had tactical nuclear missiles in Cuba. Furthermore, they had local command authority to fire them to halt an invasion. Had American troops stormed the beaches of Cuba, the outnumbered Soviets certainly would have used their nuclear weapons and then Kennedy would have had no choice but to retaliate with American nuclear devices. The response would likely have been an attack on Soviet soil (Wiersma and Larson 1997).

I had an officer like Robert Kennedy on my senior staff. He was rather unique, too, in that he had been passed over for promotion several times and was not trying to "make points" with the boss. He was the one staff member I could count on to question every initial position and to take the opposing view in most discussions. Although I encouraged this type of open debate, he was the only staff member who consistently helped us to see obvious flaws in our reasoning.

> *"Above all, leadership is a position of servanthood. Leadership is also a position of debt; it is a forfeiture of rights."*
> —*Max DePree*

Senior leadership is lonely and the single chief encourages highly filtered information. J. Oswald Sanders argues that because the leader must always be ahead of his followers, he lives with loneliness (Sanders 1994).

> Two days before the scheduled Normandy invasion of World War II involving more than two million men, General Eisenhower, the Supreme Allied Commander, received the final briefing from his staff. "When they had finished asking questions there was silence which lasted for a full five minutes while General Eisenhower sat on a sofa before the bookcase which filled the end of the room. I never realized before the loneliness and isolation of a Commander at a time when such a momentous decision has to be taken, with full knowledge that failure or success rests on his judgment alone" (Puryear, 1971, 358).

McClelland's Need Theory proposes that senior leaders have a higher need for achievement and power than for affiliation (McClelland 1962). Top leaders find it difficult to have close friends within their organizations and this often leads to a sense of isolation. When a top leader has a problem, whom can he turn to? Senior leaders do not have the luxury of participating in casual banter around the water cooler or debate over lunch about the newest customer's proclivities. Usually, his information is received in formal briefings that are highly filtered and formally structured. Those involved in the briefings are mindful of protecting their own turf and no one wants to appear to be a "loose cannon." Only safe solutions will be presented lest one appears to be "reckless." There is little "thinking outside the box." Contentious information, or where there is disagreement between staff members, will be excluded from the briefing if it is too difficult to explain under blistering questioning. Unless he really digs, the single chief will receive a highly polished briefing that has been filtered down to the non-controversial essentials. As a result, the single chief will be shutoff from creative but unconventional solutions to problems. Organizational growth, if it happens at all, will be by incrementalism and not by the great leaps required in today's competitive environment. Single chief organizations will become relics on the information superhighway.

Greenleaf argues that the burden of indecisiveness is greater than the benefit of decisiveness. In other words, when faced with making all the decisions, the single chief tends toward indecisiveness. Certainly, there are benefits to having a single decision maker who can unilaterally make all the calls. However, the weight of decision-making hangs heavy on most top leaders.

The single chief limits the opportunities for growth for new leaders. One of the most important functions of senior leaders is to train junior leaders. If the boss makes all the decisions, how will middle and first level managers ever learn? Unless the top leader delegates accountability along with responsibility and authority, junior leaders will never learn from their mistakes as well as their successes. This requires a senior leader who has a strong sense of security and self-confidence. Insecure leaders will play their cards close to the chest. Power results from having all the information. Only self-assured leaders will take the risk to allow their subordinates to make mistakes. Max DePree argues that one of the most important responsibilities of a top leader is to prepare other leaders who will look to the future of the organization (DePree 1989). That means training junior leaders to assume senior leadership responsibilities while the top leader is still with the organization to guide and instruct.

The single leader is grossly overburdened with busyness, which destroys creativity. When I was a staff officer in the Pentagon, I often briefed the senior military and civilian leadership regarding my program. These senior leaders had appointment calendars that began at 7:30 a.m. and extended often until late in the evening. Every 30-minute block was scheduled with a different briefing. Some briefings were simply informational, i.e., status reports on progress within a project or program. But many of the briefings were decision briefs, i.e., aimed at obtaining a decision at the conclusion of the brief (and hopefully, for the briefer, the decision that he recommended!). When was there time to think, to be creative, to plan for the future? The answer is, of course, there was no time!

Time management is difficult for everyone. This is especially true for someone who has the additional burden of making all the decisions.

In his national best-selling book on personal change and management, *The Seven Habits of Highly Effective People* (1989), Covey argues that the key to effective time management is to organize and execute around priorities. He divides the way we spend our time into four quadrants. Quadrant I includes those activities that are *urgent* and *important*; these include crises, pressing problems, and deadline-driven projects. Quadrant II activities are *not urgent* but *important*; these include planning, relationship-building, and recognizing new opportunities. Quadrant III activities are *urgent* but *not important*, including some mail, interruptions, some phone calls, meaningless meetings and the like. Quadrant IV includes time-wasters like busy work, some mail and phone calls, or just daydreaming. He suggests that for most people, up to 90% of their time is spent in Quadrant I reacting to crises and deadlines with the remaining 10% spent on trivia (Quadrant IV). Completely neglected by most senior leaders are those all-important Quadrant II activities that contribute to effective leadership of a vision-driven organization. The single chief is assured of following this pattern.

An organization that relies upon a single chief for all decisions will often come to a screeching halt when that person leaves. Even when a single chief announces plans to retire, how do you prepare junior leaders to assume decision-making authority when they have never been allowed that prerogative in the past? What if the single chief is incapacitated by a stroke or heart attack? What if she drops dead in the parking lot? What if the boss announces that he is moving to another CEO position? In any of these situations, the organization dominated by a single chief will experience significant disruption in operations while staff members try to sort out how to keep the ship afloat until the new skipper arrives. Needless to say, during what may be an extended period of time, the organization is going nowhere.

With a single decision-maker calling all the shots, there is no leadership by persuasion. Therefore the senior leader does not have the growth opportunity that results from learning to present his case in such a manner that others are persuaded by the merits of the argument. Junior leaders do not grow because they are shut out of the learning process. We have a lose-lose situation!

Finally, the single chief model emphasizes management and not leadership. *Control* receives priority over leadership. Control is a function of management. Leadership requires *motivating* people to do what you want done. Therefore the single chief is a manager not a leader.

Servant Leadership in Business

Greenleaf seems to have developed his leadership theory independent of any knowledge of Deming's model; however, the similarities are striking. Greenleaf calls for a new business ethic where excellence is the motivator: in service and products. Not only should businesses focus on producing better products but also they should consider themselves social assets as institutions. Social responsibility, or demonstration of social consciousness, through special care of the environment, supporting volunteer programs, enforcement of recycling programs and other "responsible" programs have been quite popular in American industry in the last decade. Examples of how the company is involved in such activities are often prominently featured in annual reports to stockholders.

Excellence, of course, is the cornerstone of quality leadership. Deming's system of profound knowledge aims toward transformation of the individual who, in turn, will transform their organizations (Deming 1982). He does not directly address corporate social responsibility but states that the transformed individual will perceive new meaning in life and in relationships with others. Deming's focus was more on providing superior products in environments that provide meaningful work while respecting the dignity of each human being. Some might call that social responsibility, too.

Deming's dictum to remove obstacles to joy in work is consistent with Greenleaf's belief that the work exists for the person as much as the person exists for the work.

Ever-increasing government regulation of business was counterproductive to Greenleaf. He contended that regulation diminished the individual's conscience to govern. Regulation promotes a rule utilitarian ethical viewpoint where if your actions are not illegal then they are permitted. Why worry about self-governing when the federal/state/local government will control what you can and cannot do anyway? I liken it to the way Naval aviators (Navy and Marine) would explain the difference in operations between Air Force pilots and themselves. They contended that Air Force pilots would not do anything that was not authorized in writing. Naval aviators, on the other hand, could do anything unless it was specifically prohibited. Their belief, naïve as it may have been, was that they were the creative, innovative ones, while their brethren in blue were the hidebound bureaucrats. Although Paul reminds us of the value of the law, "I would not have known sin except through the law" (Romans 7:7), excessive regulation tends to not only hinder economic growth but also to discourage ontological (i.e., based on an enduring set of universal principles and precepts) decision-making.

> *"There is a loftier ambition than merely to stand high in the world. It is to stoop down and lift mankind a little higher."*
> —*Henry Van Dyke*

Applying Greenleaf's servant leadership model to our 21st century businesses will result in leaders with great intuitive insight whose major talent will be as team-builders. Their companies will be models of excellence in products and socially responsible members of their communities.

We now turn our attention to a new model for Christian leadership suggested by the research of George Barna and others.

8

A Model for Christian Leadership

"A Christian leader is someone who is called by God to lead and possess virtuous character and effectively motivates, mobilizes resources, and directs people toward fulfillment of a jointly embraced vision from God."
—*George Barna*

George Barna, in his book, *The Second Coming of the Church* (1998), sounds a clarion call for the church. He states that, "After nearly two decades of studying Christian churches in America, I'm convinced that the typical church as we know it today has a rapidly expiring shelf life" (Barna 1998, 1). He contends that the church in America today is paralyzed by the absence of godly leaders. His contribution to the study of leadership is not just confined to the church, as I believe he has identified traits, competencies, and leadership types that are applicable to all types of organizations and consistent with the model of leader as servant.

Essentials for Christian Leaders

In spite of his dire warning, Barna contends that there *is* good news. He believes that God has provided the leaders needed for "the rebirthing of the Christian faith in America" but that these leaders are not often recognized or mobilized (Barna 1998, x). How then *do* we identify these leaders?

True Christian leaders are distinguished from all others by three essentials: their *calling*, *character*, and leadership *competencies*.

> *"The first responsibility of a leader is to define reality."*
> —*Max DePree*

Barna contends that Christian leaders have an awareness of God's call upon their lives to lead. They know that they did not just find themselves in leadership positions by random chance but rather they recognize that God has equipped them with certain characteristics and qualities that suit them for leadership. They have an inclination to lead. Although they don't mind being a follower, they prefer to lead. They are more comfortable when they are in charge. They perceive reality differently from non-leaders. They see the possibilities while others see only the problems. They can appreciate the beauty of a leafless maple tree on a hillside silhouetted against an autumn sky while non-leaders see only the single, brown leaf hanging precariously from an intermediate branch. They naturally influence others by force of their personalities, communication skills and ideas.

They seek each other out as companions, as top leadership is lonely. Although these leaders receive external acclaim they possess internal strength. They derive joy from leading. Leadership is not a burden to them but provides intrinsic value and motivation by the very act of leading.

Distinguishing Traits

Barna contends that Christian leaders have distinguishing traits, as displayed in Figure 8-1. These traits are more relational then the leadership traits identified by Greenleaf as necessary for servant leaders, i.e., initiative, intelligence, foresight, and perception.

Figure 8-1

Character Qualities of Godly Leaders

- Honesty
- Loyalty
- Perseverance
- Trustworthiness
- Courage
- Humility
- Sensitivity
- Teachability
- Optimism
- Consistency
- Energetic
- Faithfulness
- Self-controlled
- Loving
- Wise
- Discerning
- Patient
- Encouraging

The leadership traits identified by Barna appear to be historically consistent with those traits identified by the early Christian church as necessary for leaders. This is evidenced in Paul's Second Epistle to Timothy.

In about A.D. 66, the Apostle Paul, wrote a letter of encouragement from a Roman prison to a young pastor named Timothy. In this letter, Paul reminded Timothy of the leadership traits required of Christian leaders. These traits include:

- *courage* ("For God has not given us a spirit of fear, but of power and of love and of a sound mind. You therefore, my son, be strong in the grace that is in Christ Jesus." 2 Timothy 1:7, 2:1)
- *perseverance* ("You therefore must endure hardship as a good soldier of Jesus Christ." 2 Timothy 2:3)
- *faithfulness, trustworthiness* ("This is a faithful saying: For if we also died with Him, we shall also live with Him. If we endure, we shall also reign with Him. If we deny Him, He also will deny us. If we are faithless, He remains faithful; He cannot deny Himself." 2 Timothy 2:11-13)
- *wisdom* ("Be diligent to present yourself approved to God, a worker who does not need to be ashamed, rightly dividing the word of truth." 2 Timothy 2:15)
- *self-control* ("Flee also youthful lusts; but pursue righteousness, faith, love, peace with those who call on the Lord out of a pure heart." 2 Timothy 2:22)
- *humility* ("And a servant of the Lord must not quarrel but be gentle to all, able to teach, patient, in humility correcting those who are in opposition..." 2 Timothy 2:24, 25)

These same traits that Paul identified as essential to Christian leaders may be found in the character qualities of Godly leaders, as listed in Figure 8-1.

Types of Leaders

Barna has identified from his research certain competencies that Christian leaders possess. They articulate a Godly vision while developing, coaching and motivating people. They do not shy from conflict but rather spearhead conflict resolution. They communicate truth, principles, and plans effectively and with conviction. They do not close-hold authority and responsibility but are eager delegators. These traits and competencies, and as dictated by the situation, are manifested in four types of leaders:

- Directing leaders
- Strategic leaders
- Team-building leaders
- Operational leaders

Directing leaders are required where follower competency is low and the task is very difficult or ambiguous. These leaders are value-driven visionaries who are passionate about their task or cause. They act as a catalyst for team action while motivating people intrinsically by constantly reinforcing the value of their work. They can be assertive, when required, while respecting the individual dignity and worth of their followers.

Strategic leaders are necessary for developing synthesis for a shared vision for the organization. They exhibit wisdom, reflection, and patience. They are pragmatic and well prepared while empowering followers with the authority to carry out decision-making functions for the organization.

Team-building leaders are necessary at all levels but especially with smaller groups of competent and committed followers. They are skilled at developing relationships and blending talents to complete cross-functional tasks. Their optimism and enthusiasm are contagious. They are tactful and flexible recognizing that each member of the team brings different skills and talents that need to be nurtured and encouraged for the benefit of the team's success.

Operational leaders are essentially managers who implement the strategies of the strategic leaders. They have exceptional organizing skills that create process and order while focusing on the details. They support the plans and policies of senior leadership with accuracy and efficiency.

Barna contends that these four types of leaders are present in the most effective organizations. The absence of any one of these types will decrease the efficiency and capacity of the organization. If one or more of the types of leaders are not available to the organization, then someone must assume the missing role(s). Unfortunately, too many organizations look to a single individual to perform all four leadership roles. Although some exceptional individuals may be able to pull this off for a short period of time, burnout is inevitable. The key to success is to identify men and women with the character qualities and skills necessary for the four types of leaders and to train them to assume those roles. An alternative suggested by Barna, is to delegate specific functions normally performed by a leader type to individuals with gifts in those specific areas. The least effective but most commonly used alternative is for the organization to "simply do the best it can" without the skills of the missing leader type (Barna 1998, 118).

Barna concludes that Christian lay leaders are emerging to assume leadership roles that were formally performed by clergy as they answer God's call on their lives. He contends that senior leaders must seek out such potential leaders and provide them the training and tools necessary to assume these vital leadership positions for the good of the entire Church.

Barna's research is important to our study of leadership since it confirms what we are seeing elsewhere, namely that the character qualities of leaders is critical to building all-important relationships with followers. The *National Survey on Public Leadership*, referred to in Chapter 1, concluded that "character is perceived to be more important than competence in solving today's public problems" (Goodman 1999, 2). I believe this statement is equally true in for-profit businesses as well as in private, not-for-profit institutions.

With this review of traditional leadership theories, quality leadership, Greenleaf's servant leadership, and Barna's Christian leadership model, we now turn to a detailed examination of the leadership approach of the One who modeled the concept of leader as servant, Jesus of Nazareth.

9

Jesus, A Model for Leadership

"Jesus was God centered."
—Richard White

Jesus of Nazareth, the Second Person of the Trinity, is worthy of our study as Savior and LORD but seldom do we study Him for his leadership style and attributes. Was He a great leader whose style of leadership is worthy of emulation in today's world? The remainder of this book is devoted to proving that the answer to that question is emphatically, Yes!

So far, we have studied the traditional models for understanding leadership, the contributions of quality leadership, servant leadership as defined by Greenleaf, and a model for Christian leaders. We will now examine the servant as leader as lived out in the life of Jesus. He built a values-driven organization based on Godly principles that celebrated the dignity and worth of each individual. This "organization" has not only endured but has greatly prospered and expanded over the last two thousand years often in the face of persecution and determined opposition.

What can we learn from the way Jesus led? How was He able to take a dozen men, none who could be considered among the learned men of the day, and ignite a firestorm in their hearts so that they would instruct not only the secular leaders of their time but countless millions throughout the ages since? Let's find out He did it!

Jesus' Heritage

When studying someone's life, and especially their leadership style, it is helpful to have an image of that person in order to have a better understanding of who they are and what has molded them into the person they became. We can look at a portrait of Lincoln or Napoleon and begin to gain insight into the man behind the mask. I have hanging in my office a Alexander Gardner photograph of President Lincoln taken near the end of the American Civil War and coincidentally near the end of his life. As I stare into the dark, sad eyes of one of our greatest presidents, I am almost overwhelmed with his compassion. Here is a man who carries the pain of each grieving mother on both sides of that awful conflict. On the other hand, looking at a portrait of Napoleon, one is struck by the proud eyes and up-thrust chin of a diminutive man stretching to make himself taller and thus appear more important. Each image says something about the man and how he led others.

Who was Jesus and what did He look like? Unfortunately, we do not have a photograph or contemporary painting of Him. But we can gain an understating of His appearance by what evidence is available—and some of that is quite remarkable!

His genealogy is laid out in the Gospels of Matthew and Luke with the two writers taking different approaches. Matthew follows the legal Jewish system of the father's genealogy by tracing the lineage of Jesus from the founder of the Jewish race (Abraham) through his earthly father, Joseph. Matthew is quick to point out that Joseph is not Jesus' actual father but as he is writing for a largely Jewish audience, his purpose is to demonstrate the royal lineage of Jesus and that He is the promised Messiah. Luke takes a different approach. He ascends the family line all the way to Adam thereby identifying Jesus universally with the entire human race. By studying these two genealogies we can gain some insight into Jesus physical appearance.

The great artistic masters generally depicted Jesus as a fair-skinned European like themselves. In fact, Jesus was a tradesman, a craftsman of His day who worked with wood and stone. He learned His earthly father's trade as a carpenter (or stone mason) and would have assisted Joseph from an early age. He had rough, strong, calloused hands and a lean, muscular body. He was accustomed to working in the hot Mediterranean sun stripped to the waist and drenched in sweat. His natural olive-shaded skin tone would have been even darker due to a perpetually deep tan from His outdoor work. In short, He looked like a Jew!

However, the genealogies provide other interesting clues about Jesus' appearance. Both sides of Jesus' earthly heritage have King David as an ancestor thus confirming His royal lineage. David's great-grandmother was Rahab, a Canaanite from the line of Ham, the second son of Noah (Genesis 10:6). The descendents of Canaan settled in modern day Israel. Cush, one of Ham's other sons, settled in modern day Ethiopia while Put settled in modern day Libya (Hayford 1991). David's grandmother was Ruth, a Moabite, another Canaanite tribe. With this much African blood by American standards, David could be considered black.

King Solomon was David's son by a Hamitic woman, Bathsheba (daughter of Sheba), an African. In the Messianic line of Jesus, through Joseph, four women are mentioned in the genealogy: Tamar, Rahab, Ruth, and Bathsheba (Matthew 1). All four of these women are descendants of Ham, an African. Jesus' mother, Mary, was also a descendant of Tamar, Rahab, and Ruth. Clearly, Jesus did not look like a Northern European. Again, He looked like a Jew!

In this age where technology reigns supreme, I believe that God, in His infinite wisdom, mercy, and grace, knowing what a stiff-necked people we are, has left us another important clue, a "snapshot" of Jesus on his burial cloth. The Shroud of Turin, bears the ventral and dorsal image of a scourged, crucified man and what appear to be bloodstains that coincide with Christ's crucifixion wounds. The 14½-foot long, 3½-foot wide linen cloth has been kept in the city of Turin, Italy since 1578.

Although millions have viewed the faint image on the shroud, it was not until the close of the 19th century with the invention of the modern camera that God's gift became readily apparent. In 1898, Secondo Pia, an Italian amateur photographer, took the first photograph of the Shroud of Turin. Pia's negative image of the Shroud clearly revealed the image of a crucified man (Wilson 1996).

Ian Wilson, probably the best-known Shroud researcher, has written extensively on the sacred linen over the past forty years. His book, *The Blood and the Shroud* (1998), was written specifically to address the 1988 conclusion by a team of radiocarbon dating experts that the Shroud was a fake. They concluded that the linen cloth dated from approximately AD 1325, give or take sixty-five years. Obviously, this astonishing finding meant that the Shroud could not possibly be the burial cloth of the historical Jesus. To say this rocked many faithful Shroud watchers is an understatement! Five years later, another scientist working independently, would make a discovery that would challenge the radiocarbon dating conclusion.

In 1993, Dr. Leoncio Garza-Valdes of the University of Texas, a pediatrician and microbiology specialist discovered "Lichenothelia varnish," or bioplastic coating, around the linen threads of the Shroud. This natural-forming material, unnoticed by the team of radiocarbon scientists, would cause the fibers of the Shroud to show a much younger date than they actually were. Needless to say, this finding has created an uproar among the scientific community and has called into question the accuracy of the 1988 conclusion.

In 1998, Alan D. Adler, a renowned expert in blood chemistry who investigated the Shroud of Turin for the Vatican, established that the shroud image was that of a person, and the blood came from violently inflicted wounds. He said blood flowing from wounds has a different chemistry than blood flowing in veins. But he said he couldn't prove whether the image on the shroud was Christ's.

> "We know for sure it's human blood and it came from a man who died a traumatic death," Adler said in a 1998 interview. "There's no laboratory test for 'Christness.'" (*New York Times*, June 13, 2000)

A persistent theory has been that the image was somehow painted on the linen cloth. However, modern technology has allowed scientists to measure the depth of the image across the entire length of the cloth. They have discovered an unexplainable uniformity in the depth of the image in the linen fibers. A painted image would, of course, have varying depth as the paint soaked into the cloth. To some, the image seems to have been created by an instantaneous flash of bright light burning the image on the surrounding cloth. The current consensus is that *how* the image appeared on the Shroud is unexplainable (Wilson 1998).

Figure 9-1 depicts the head of the image on the Shroud. One can clearly see the traces of blood (light-colored in this negative image) from the forehead, a swollen and probably broken nose, puffy eyes, and other evidence of a severe beating. If this is the image of Jesus of Nazareth, as I believe it is, then we have a very clear picture of what he looked like. If it is not, we still have a good idea of the appearance of this Jewish carpenter as we turn to study His unique style of leadership.

Figure 9-1 The Shroud of Turin (head image)

Servant Leader Defined

There are three types of New Testament leaders: servant leader (or deacon), steward leader (or manager), and steersman leader (or overseer). The steersman leader comes from the Greek *kypernesis*, and refers to one who acts as pilot or helmsman (steers). The steward leader comes from the Greek word *oikonomos*. This refers to a household manager. The third type is the servant leader or *diakonia*. This term is typically used when referring to selfless ministry such as that performed by the first deacons (see Acts 6:1-6).

What distinguishes a servant leader from all other leaders? *It is the condition of the leader's heart.* The servant leader:

- Recognizes and meets the needs of his followers
- Puts the needs of his followers above his own
- Loves those he leads

A servant leader actively seeks to know the needs of his followers. He looks for unspoken signs as well as verbalized requests. He looks out for their future and helps to plan their growth. His decision-making is motivated by what is best for his followers and not what will benefit him. Where there is a conflict between promoting his own good and the good of his followers, he always defers to the followers best interest.

Some will be surprised to learn that this characteristic was highly esteemed by General Eisenhower in his senior leaders during World War II. Six days after the allied invasion of Europe, Army Chief of Staff General George Marshall asked,

> "Eisenhower, you've chosen all these commanders or accepted those we sent from Washington. What's the principal quality you look for?" General Eisenhower later noted, "Without even thinking I said 'selflessness'" (Puryear, 1971, 71).

A servant leader loves his followers with an *agape* love that

> "denotes an undefeatable benevolence and unconquerable good will that always seeks the highest good of the other person, no

matter what he does. It is the self-giving love that gives freely without asking anything in return, and does not consider the worth of its object" (*Spirit Filled Life Bible* 1991, 1994).

A servant leader's motivation is to serve his followers, to see them grow, and when necessary, to sacrifice for them. His chief concern is always their best interest and not his own.

His Guiding Principles

In Chapter 5, we examined the need for a successful organization to have a set of guiding principles to provide the purpose, direction, and rules of behavior for members of the organization. Guiding principles provide the answers to three questions:

1. Who are we? (mission)
2. Who do we hope to become? (vision)
3. How will we treat our customers (internal and external) on our journey toward our vision? (values)

Did Jesus build his "organization" on a set of guiding principles? Yes, He did! Let's examine those guiding principles.

Vision. The vision for an organization provides its direction. It is future oriented and must be shared by members of the organization in order to be effective and perpetuated. It provides a desired end-state that may never be reached yet causes the members of the organization to stretch toward its image.

Jesus often communicated to His disciples through stories and parables what the kingdom of heaven was like. All of these, however, pointed to the "new heaven and a new earth" (Isaiah 65:17) when Jesus will return to earth to reign as King of Kings and LORD of LORDS.

> Then the sign of the Son of Man will appear
> in heaven, and then all the tribes of the earth
> will mourn, and they will see the Son of Man
> coming on the clouds of heaven with power
> and great glory. And He will send His angels
> with a great sound of a trumpet, and they will
> gather together His elect from the four
> winds, from one end of heaven to the other
> (Matthew 24:30, 31).

Successful leaders will reiterate their vision time and
again until it truly becomes a shared vision. Theodore
Hesburgh, past-president of Notre Dame University, has
said that a leader cannot blow an uncertain trumpet (see 1
Corinthians 14:8). The leader must be sure of his vision and
continually reinforce it to his followers. Jesus reminded His
disciples of the coming kingdom often. We see this
recorded in the 19th chapter of Matthew in His response to a
question from Peter,

> Then Peter answered and said to Him, "See,
> we have left all and followed You. Therefore
> what shall we have?" So Jesus said to them,
> "Assuredly I say to you, that in the regenera-
> tion, when the Son of Man sits on the throne
> of His glory, you who have followed Me will
> also sit on twelve thrones, judging the twelve
> tribes of Israel" (Matthew 19:27, 28).

He warns his followers against following a false vision:

> "Take heed that no one deceives you. For
> many will come in My name, saying, 'I am

the Christ,' and will deceive many"
(Matthew 24:4, 5).

And again He instructs them as to what the true vision
will be:

> "Then the sign of the Son of Man will appear
> in heaven, and then all the tribes of the earth
> will mourn, and they will see the Son of Man
> coming on the clouds of heaven with power
> and great glory. And He will send His angels
> with a great sound of a trumpet, and they will
> gather together His elect from the four
> winds, from one end of heaven to the other"
> (Matthew 24:30, 31).

The proof that this vision was truly shared by His disciples is borne out in their lives and deaths. The best evidence of the bodily resurrection of Jesus is the dramatic change that it had upon His followers. Consider the state of Jesus' disciples following His crucifixion and burial. They were huddled together behind closed doors fearful of "the Jews." At any moment they expected to be arrested and hauled off for execution, as had their LORD. They were dejected and defeated. "We believed He was the One, the promised Messiah and now He is dead and gone forever!" they must have lamented. And then something happened to change them. Suddenly, they were boldly proclaiming His truths in the streets and before the very judges who had condemned their leader to a cross. What could have brought about this dramatic change? The only logical explanation is that they had seen the resurrected Jesus. They had touched His nail-pierced hands and feet and had put their hands in the wound in His side. They knew that His words, "In my Father's house are many mansions; if it were not so, I would have told you. I go to prepare a place for you," (John 14:2) were true! No one will die for a lie. These men knew that everything Jesus had told them was true. His vision became their vision. And they would proclaim that vision throughout the rest of their lives with boldness and courage even unto their own martyrdom.

Mission. An organization's mission represents its purpose, its reason for being. It is reflective of what we do now. The mission is consistent with an organization's vision and represents a temporary condition that will be transcended as the organization moves toward its visionary end-state. Jesus chose to publicly declare His mission in His hometown of Nazareth soon after He had returned from His time of preparation in the wilderness.

> So He came to Nazareth, where He had been brought up. And as His custom was, He went into the synagogue on the Sabbath day, and stood up to read. And He was handed the book of the prophet Isaiah. And when He had opened the book, He found the place where it was written:
> "The Spirit of the LORD is upon Me,
> Because He has anointed Me
> To preach the gospel to the poor;
> He has sent Me to heal the brokenhearted,
> To proclaim liberty to the captives
> And recovery of sight to the blind,
> To set at liberty those who are oppressed;
> To proclaim the acceptable year of the LORD."
>
> Then he closed the book, and gave it back to the attendant and sat down. And the eyes of all who were in the synagogue were fixed on Him (Luke 4:16-20).

Jesus was declaring to those who would be most skeptical of His claims, since they had seen Him growing up, that He was the promised *mashiach*, the Messiah. Later, He repeats His claim in a dramatic and unmistakable way to the Jewish leaders.

> "You search the Scriptures, for in them you think you have eternal life; and these are they which testify of Me" (John 5:39).

As with vision, leaders must continually drive home the mission of the organization. Jesus does this immediately following His teaching on values (the Beatitudes) where He makes clear His mission was *not* to bring a new doctrine or set of laws,

> "Do not think that I came to destroy the Law or the Prophets. I did not come to destroy but to fulfill" (Matthew 5:17).

Jesus goes on to describe that His mission was to *complete* the Law and the Prophets; i.e., He was the promised Messiah who, in John Eldredge's words, came "...to give you back your heart and set you free." (Eldredge 2003, 51) He then began to explain the Law in a way the people had never heard before with a series of teachings that began, "You have heard that it was said ... but *I* say to you ..." (see Matthew 5:21-48, *emphasis added*).

Again, we can see Jesus reiterating His mission to the messengers from John the Baptist, who asked Him,

> "Are You the Coming One, or do we look for another?" Jesus answered and said to them, "Go and tell John the things which you hear and see: The blind see and the lame walk; the

lepers are cleansed and the deaf hear; the
dead are raised up and the poor have the
gospel preached to them" (Matthew 11:3-5).

Jesus made it clear that He understood His mission was
to the Jews first. He also knew that many Jews would reject
Him and that He would extend His kingdom to the Gentiles.

But He answered and said, "I was not sent
except to the lost sheep of the house of
Israel" (Matthew 15:24).

Later, He tells the Jewish leaders two parables. The first
is about a landowner who sends his servants, and finally his
son, to collect the rent due from his tenants only to have
them beaten and killed. The second concerns a wedding
feast whose invited guests were unwilling to attend. Jesus
concludes with these warnings:

"Therefore I say to you, the kingdom of God
will be taken from you and given to a nation
bearing the fruits of it." "For many are
called, but few are chosen" (Matthew 21:43,
22:14).

Near the end of His earthly ministry He reassured His
followers that they would be empowered to carry on His
mission when He had gone.

"Most assuredly, I say to you, he who
believes in Me, the works that I do he will do
also; and greater works than these he will do,
because I go to My Father" (John 14:12).

Values. An organization's values are those norms that set the conduct of the members of the organization apart. "This is how will we treat our customers and each other as we move toward our vision for the future." As norms, they are often unspoken but accepted by the members of the organization as "the way we do things around here." In order to be effective, publicly declared organizational values must be consistent with the conduct of members of the organization beginning with senior management. When what we say is not what we do then there is dissonance between our values (what we say) and our norms (what we do). An attitude of "Do what I say and not what I do," will surely destroy any values that are not consistent with organizational norms. Senior leaders must carefully select organizational values since once publicly declared they become the rod by which members will measure the veracity of organizational policies and procedures. An organization that declares its values and then does not follow them will destroy the loyalty of its members. If you say that you will always be truthful with your customers and with each other and then concoct excuses why an important shipment will be late, you may not only lose a customer but you will severely undermine your values.

Several professors from the Naval War College attended a course at IBM's Market-Driven Quality Institute some years ago. We were not only instructed in Big Blue's approach to quality but in formal presentations and informal conversations we learned of IBM's values especially how they considered the interests of their people above all else. "We take care of our own," was often repeated in the classroom and at the coffee shop. When you went to work for IBM you expected that as long as you did your job to the best of your ability you were assured of lifetime employment. Downsizing and restructuring were new corporate strategies but unheard of at IBM. Big Blue was a way of life. It was much more than just a job.

A woman described to me how she had been with a team from New York on a business trip to California when a member of the team received a phone call that a close family member was gravely ill. Since it was late in the evening, this team member was unable to obtain a flight home until sometime the next morning. "And do you know that they sent a corporate jet to pick her up and fly her home so that she could be with her loved one?, she declared. "We take care of our own!" All of us who heard the story were very impressed with the commitment to their organizational values IBM leadership demonstrated by this incident.

About a year later, the major shakeup of IBM described in Chapter 1 began with not only a change in top leadership but for the first time massive layoffs. The damage to IBM's values and the destruction of employee loyalty as a result of these layoffs are incalculable. The message to senior management is this: select your organizational values with great care because you may have to live up to them!

Jesus first declared His organizational values beginning with His teaching known as the Beatitudes (Matthew 5-7). He declared that He and His followers were to exemplify:
- Humility (5:3)
- Willingness to suffer persecution (5:10)
- Seeking to follow God's commandments (5:19)

- Genuinely righteous behavior not false piety (5:20)
- Living a life of prayer (6:10, 13)
- Placing spiritual values above temporal values (6:33)
- Obeying the revealed will of God (7:21)

Today, most of us have at least heard reference to these values but when Jesus spoke them they were considered radical concepts.

> And so it was, when Jesus had ended these sayings, that the people were astonished at His teaching, for he taught them as one having authority, and not as the scribes. (Matthew 7:28, 29)

These radical values were lived out by Jesus and transmitted to His followers in word and deed. They have been transforming His followers ever since.

Jesus did have a set of guiding principles for the organization that He intended to build. He articulated those principles clearly and consistently to his followers but especially to His disciples to whom He would entrust the future of the organization.

In the next chapter we will examine Jesus' strategy for implementing His vision.

10

Jesus' Five-Phase Strategy

Shepherd the flock of God which is among you, serving as
overseers, not by compulsion but willingly, not for
dishonest gain but eagerly; nor as being lords over those
entrusted to you, but being examples to the flock.
—2 Peter 5:2,3

As we discussed in Chapter 1, leaders are responsible for *doing the right things.* This includes not only insuring that their products, both now and in the future, meet the needs of their customers, but that they also have sound strategies for delivering those products, developing new products and markets, and for continued organizational growth.

We should not be surprised that Jesus had a five-phase strategy for preparing, deploying, and growing His organization. Those five phases were:

I. Preparation
II. Picking potential leaders

III. Enablement
IV. Empowerment
V. Deployment

Let's look at each of these phases in detail.

Phase I: Preparation

Jesus understood that before He could create His organization, He had to prepare Himself. From the Scriptures we have scant information regarding Jesus' early life but from what we do have we know that He was considered wise even as a child.

> And the Child grew and became strong in spirit, filled with wisdom, and the grace of God was upon Him (Luke 2:40).

He loved to go to the temple in Jerusalem when His family would come up for the annual feasts and sit among the learned scholars and participate in their dialectic discussion.

> Now so it was that after three days they found Him in the temple, sitting in the midst of the teachers, both listening to them and asking them questions. And all who heard Him were astonished at His understanding and answers (Luke 2:46, 47).

Growing up in the household of His earthly father, Joseph, Jesus would have apprenticed as a carpenter. Although He knew all of His life what His life's mission was to be, it was not until He was about 30 years old that His Father *called* Jesus into His ministry. He symbolically announced the start of His public ministry by submitting to baptism by His cousin John.

> Then Jesus came from Galilee to John at the
> Jordan to be baptized by him. And John tried
> to prevent Him, saying, "I need to be
> baptized by You, and are You coming to
> me?" But Jesus answered and said to him,
> "Permit it to be so now, for thus it is fitting
> for us to fulfill all righteousness." Then he
> allowed Him (Matthew 3:13-15).

This public sacrament demonstrated to all Jesus' willingness to submit to the will of His Father even though
John's baptism was one of repentance and confession of sin.
Although He was sinless, Jesus was affirming the necessity
for confession and repentance for entry into the kingdom of
heaven. God the Father honored Jesus' faithfulness by pour-
ing out the Holy Spirit upon Him "like a dove" and unmis-
takably calling Him out.

> And suddenly a voice came from heaven,
> saying, "This is My beloved Son, in whom I
> am well pleased" (Matthew 3:17).

Following His baptism, "Jesus was led by the Spirit into
the wilderness to be tempted by the devil (Matthew 4:1).
During this intense period of testing, Jesus applied the
power of scripture to deflect the temptations of Satan. Since
the beginning of time, the tempter has used a three-pronged
attack on men and women: physically, emotionally, and
spiritually. After fasting for forty days and nights, Jesus was
very hungry. Knowing this was a weakness and seeing an
opening, Satan first attacked Jesus with physical temptation.

Now when the tempter came to Him, he said,

"If You are the Son of God, command that
these stones become bread" (Matthew 4:3).

Jesus responded by quoting scripture,

> But He answered and said, "It is written,
> 'Man shall not live by bread alone, but by
> every word that proceeds from the mouth of
> God'" (Matthew 4:4).

Jesus learned, in a very practical sense, the power of
God's word to deflect and defeat Satan's intentions.

Thwarted in the physical realm, Satan next turned to
emotional temptation by trying to force Jesus into proving
His Messiahship.

> "If you are the Son of God, throw Yourself
> down. For it is written: He shall give His
> angels charge over you,' and 'In their hands
> they shall bear you up, Lest you dash your
> foot against a stone'" (Matthew 4:6).

Again, Jesus responded with scripture,

> Jesus said to him, "It is written again, 'You
> shall not tempt the LORD your God'"
> (Matthew 4:7).

Finally, Satan showed his trump card, spiritual temptation.

> Again, the devil took Him up on an exceed-
> ingly high mountain, and showed Him all the
> kingdoms of the world and their glory. And
> he said to Him, "All these things I will give
> You if You will fall down and worship me"

(Matthew 4:8, 9).

Undeterred by Satan's attack, Jesus dismissed him with God's word ringing in his ears,

> Then Jesus said to him, "Away with you, Satan! For it is written, 'You shall worship the LORD your God, and Him only you shall serve.'" Then the devil left Him, and behold angels came and ministered to Him (Matthew 4:10, 11).

Filled with the power of the Holy Spirit and leaving Satan behind licking his wounds, Jesus returned to Galilee and began to preach in the synagogues and His reputation swelled. Soon, he returned to His hometown of Nazareth. On the Sabbath, He went to the synagogue and His presence caused quite a stir. "The son of the carpenter is here. They say he is a great preacher now!" All eyes were on Him and He was afforded the honor of reading from the scripture. He selected a scroll containing the words of the prophet Isaiah, stood up and began to read,

> "The Spirit of the LORD is upon Me,
> Because He has anointed Me
> To preach the gospel to the poor;
> He has sent Me to heal the brokenhearted,
> To proclaim liberty to the captives
> And recovery of sight to the blind,
> To set at liberty those who are oppressed;
> To proclaim the acceptable year of the LORD."
> Then He closed the book, and gave it back to the attendant and sat down. And the eyes of all who were in the synagogue were fixed on Him. And He began to say to them, "Today

this Scripture is fulfilled in your hearing"
(Luke 4:16-21).

What was He saying? Was He claiming to be the
Messiah? "Is this not Joseph's son?" (Luke 4:22b) The
people were confused, as Jesus knew they would be. He
deliberately chose the toughest place to announce the start
of His ministry, His hometown, knowing that "no prophet is
accepted in his own country" (Luke 42:4). Jesus had done
His homework. He knew where the greatest resistance to
His ministry would come from and He attacked the problem
head-on.

Jesus' time of preparation is instructive to leaders in all
types of organizations. He prepared Himself from the time
He was a small boy to obey God's calling. Although He was
not trained in the classical sense, as was his disciple Paul,
Jesus knew the scripture and the teachings of the rabbis and
could use God's word as an instrument to defeat both temporal and spiritual principalities. He waited until the time was
right to begin his life's work. He did not duck known problems and would not allow himself to be distracted.

Likewise, leaders, and those who would be leaders,
should prepare with equal diligence for positions of responsibility. Has God called you to this position or do you aspire to
leadership for selfish and self-centered reasons? Have you
prepared for this position by learning all you can about the
organization and its people, its mission, vision, and values?
Do you understand the organization's business? Do you
know the "players," both internally and externally? Do you
know the strengths and weaknesses of the organization?
What threats and opportunities are lurking in the external
environment? Have you identified major gaps in performance
between objectives, goals and actual performance? Have you
devised preliminary plans to close these gaps? Do you need
additional training? Have *you* done your homework?

Phase II: Picking Potential Leaders

We have already discussed the need for raising up new leaders and delegating to them responsibility, authority, and accountability. It is often said that one of the keys to successful top leadership is to surround yourself with highly capable people and then allow them to do their work. Jesus certainly did not heed that bit of wisdom. He picked some of the most unlikely men to follow Him and trained them to be the future leaders of His Church. None of the original twelve were learned men. Only Saul, later known as Paul, and not one of the original twelve, had received a classical education. These were laborers, men who worked with their hands. Fishermen, with big egos and fiery tempers, were chosen. He selected Simon, know as the Zealot, a Canaanite from among the people God had told the Israelites to drive out of the Promised Land and Levi, a turncoat tax collector who worked for Rome and robbed his own people! He even called Judas Iscariot who would betray Him for thirty pieces of silver.

Jesus had the unique ability to see the potential in people regardless of their outward appearance or status. He did not see what they *were* He saw what they could *become*. His only requirement was a willingness to change and grow. He would provide all the other tools necessary to do what He wanted done. "Follow me," was all he had to say but the choice remained with each man to comply. And there was a cost.

> "If anyone desires to come after Me, let him deny himself, and take up his cross, and follow Me. For whoever desires to save his life will lose it, but whoever loses his life for My sake will find it" (Matthew 16:24, 25).

Luke tells us that Jesus spent all night in prayer on a mountain before He selected the twelve from among His talmidim[2] and called them apostles (Luke 6:12, 13). These men would be the backbone of the ministry, the future leaders. They were selected with great care. God's counsel was sought and received. It was not by chance that none were from among the scribes and Pharisees. Those learned men of the day already had their minds made up—they knew the truth—had staked their reputations on it—and would not be deterred by this usurper from Galilee! Instead He chose men who could be molded into the leaders He wanted them to be. They would fail time and again, become proud, and deny they even knew Him, yet He saw their potential. He poured Himself into them that they might do His will. They were transformed by the renewing of their minds (Romans 12:2) into the leaders He knew they could become.

What about you? How do you choose your future senior leaders? What characteristics are most important to you? Is it education, a degree from a prestigious institution, the right connections, or experience? Are you able to see beyond what a person *is* to what that person can *become*? How important to you is a person's willingness to be molded into what you want them to be? What prejudices and preconceptions do you have about women as leaders, minorities as leaders, or young people as leaders? Do you seek godly counsel when selecting your future leaders? Are you willing to forgive their mistakes, to pick them up when they fail and to encourage them time and again? What can you learn from the way Jesus selected his future leaders?

Phase III: Enablement

Before you can empower your followers you must *enable* them. This means providing them with the resources (i.e., education, training, tools, equipment, time, experience) necessary to perform with a high degree of confidence the leadership functions that will be delegated to them. A couple of years ago, there were a number of stories in the press about the demise of total quality management. Several companies had tried to implement the principles of TQM only to throw up their hands in frustration a short time later when large productivity gains were not immediately forthcoming. There were a number of reasons for the "failure" of quality principles in these firms but one of the most common problems was an incomplete understanding of empowerment. In many of these firms, supervisors were instructed to turn over some of their management functions to newly formed teams of employees. The problem was that the teams were not first enabled. Management had failed to properly prepare their employees to assume the management functions now assigned to them. Of course, many of them would not succeed!

Jesus focused His time and attention on a small group of men whom He had selected from among His many followers to develop them to become His future leaders. The classical tradition, reminiscent of Plato and Aristotle, was for a select group of students to attach themselves to their rabbi—also called masters and teachers—as young boys. "To make many talmidim" is a Jewish expression from the first century that refers to the rabbi's practice of collecting disciples. Saul was trained this way by the leading teacher of his day, Gamaliel (Acts 22:3), who according to tradition had 1,000 disciples (Laan 1996). As Jesus traveled from place to place, His talmidim traveled with Him. They lived with Him while He ministered to the people and observed His values in action. They not only saw Him when He had good days, they saw Him when He had bad days. They saw Him when He was tired, when He was angry, when he was frustrated. They knew Him intimately as only one can when living with another. He taught them in small group settings and His style was very personal and by example. He lived out what He taught on a daily basis as they traveled with Him.

> *"Brethren, join in imitating me, and*
> *mark those who so live as you have an*
> *example in us."*
> —*Philippians 3:17*

Jesus taught the people using stories and parables of everyday events. They could relate to what He was saying since these things were within their realm of experience. However, He educated His future leaders with insider's knowledge of the true meaning of the stories and parables.

> Then His disciples asked Him, saying,
> "What does this parable mean?" And He
> said, "To you it has been given to know the
> mysteries of the kingdom of God, but to the
> rest it is given in parables" (Luke 8:10).

Often, He would repeat His message using different stories to insure that it was understood; e.g., the six parables on the kingdom of heaven (like weeds among wheat seed, like a mustard seed, like leaven in meal, etc.) illustrate this point. Following the parables, Jesus would explain to His disciples their meaning and ask,

> "Have you understood all these things?" They
> said to Him, "Yes, Lord" (Matthew 13:51).

Before empowering these future leaders, Jesus was providing them with all the resources they would need to assume the leadership of His ministry.

How much time do you spend with your future leaders? Have you considered the resources they will need to be able to take on the responsibility you plan to delegate to them? Do they have the education and training they need? Have you given them the time they need to learn their new responsibilities?

Phase IV: Empowerment

The root of the word empowerment is *power*. Power comes from the Greek word *exousia*, the authority or right to act. Power is the right to use *dunamis*, from which we get the English word dynamite (Vine 1997).

Empowerment is delegating decision-making responsibility to subordinates. It constitutes a transfer of process ownership from a leader to a subordinate. As discussed earlier, this means not only assigning *responsibility*, but it must also involve delegation of *authority* and *accountability*. A leader cannot hold a follower responsible for a process or function without also allowing that person to call upon the resources she will need to fulfill that responsibility. Thirdly, the empowered follower must be held accountable for the actions she takes and the outcomes she realizes through her actions. Only then does she really "own" the process.

After examining a process and deciding on what needs to be done, the second step in the Shewhart cycle for process improvement (see Chapter 5) calls for carrying out the change or test on a small scale. This is how Jesus caught His disciples. He would tell them, and then usually show them, the principle or precept He wanted them to learn. Then He would send them out to try it, on a small scale, for themselves.

The Feeding of the Five Thousand illustrates this technique. Jesus had called His disciples together and empowered them for ministry and sent them out in pairs (Mark 6:7) to preach and heal but He instructed them to go only to the Jews.

> And when He had called His twelve disciples to Him, He gave them power over unclean spirits, to cast them out, and to heal all kinds of sickness and all kinds of disease. These twelve Jesus sent out and commanded them, saying: "Do not go into the way of the Gentiles, and do not enter a city of the Samaritans. But go rather to the lost sheep of the house of Israel (Matthew 10:1, 5, 6).

Jesus sent them out in teams of two so that they could encourage one another on this their first trail. He was well aware of the proverb,

> Two are better than one,
> Because they have a good reward for their labor.
> For if they fall, one will lift up his companion (Ecclesiastes 4:9, 10).

After they returned, He debriefed them privately.

> And the apostles, when they had returned, told Him all that they had done. Then He took them and went aside privately into a deserted place belonging to the city called Bethsaida (Luke 9:10).

The twelve had completed their first independent assignment and Jesus wanted to go over all their successes and failures; what worked and what didn't work. He wanted to insure that they had learned to apply His principles correctly. He understood that they may have had some measure of success and yet not have applied the precepts precisely. They needed to get it right and He wouldn't always be there to insure that they did. He wasted no time in taking them aside to a local retreat center where they could game out every encounter, every slip, and every victory. He was interested in praising them as much as He was in critiquing them.

They barely had time to finish the "hot wash-up" when the crowds found them. Jesus did not consider the needs of the people an imposition rather He began to minister to them. With darkness approaching, the disciples suggested that Jesus send the crowds away so that they could find food and lodging for the night. Instead, Jesus took this as another opportunity to develop His future leaders.

> "You give them something to eat," He told
> them (Luke 9:13a).

In this teachable moment, He is saying, "I gave you the tools, now *you* apply them." The astonished disciples looked at one another in disbelief and said, but

> "We have no more than five loaves and two
> fish, unless we go and buy food for all these
> people" (Luke 9:13b).

The disciples only saw what *was* and not what *could be*. So, Jesus *showed* them how faith could feed five thousand people with only a few loaves of bread and a couple of fish.

In this account, we see how Jesus first enabled and then empowered His disciples by:
- instructing them
- sending them out on a trial
- critiquing them following the trial
- delegating to them again
- demonstrating by personal example when they missed

the point

After a period of further instruction including telling His disciples that He would be betrayed and put to death, Jesus sent out a larger group of disciples, again in teams of two.

> After these things the Lord appointed seventy others also, and sent them two by two before His face into every city and place where He Himself was about to go (Luke 10:1).

Occasionally the disciples encountered a situation for which they were not prepared. When so informed, Jesus would privately instruct them as to how to deal with the unusual circumstances. After empowering His followers for ministry and sending them out, Jesus came upon a group of them disputing with some scribes and surrounded by a large crowd. Jesus asked the scribes what were they discussing with His disciples and a man spoke up and said that a mute spirit possessed his son.

> "So I spoke to Your disciples, that they should cast it out, but they could not" (Mark 9:18b).

After casting out the evil spirit, Jesus took His disciples aside to instruct them.

> And when He had come into the house, His disciples asked Him privately, "Why could we not cast it out?" So He said to them, "This kind can come out by nothing but prayer and fasting" (Mark 9:28, 29).

True empowerment means that commands to followers are given through *mission-type* orders. This type of order is generalized and not prescriptive. It specifies the intended *outcome* but not the *means* for accomplishing the task. I learned this lesson early on as a young Marine second lieutenant with the parable of the flagpole.

> When you want your men to erect a flagpole, simply say, "Sergeant, put up the flagpole." Do not say, "Sergeant, assign two men to get a flagpole and two men to dig a hole 36 inches deep in such-and-such a location. Fill the hole with cement and place the pole in the wet cement and brace it until the cement dries," and so on.

Mission-type orders encourage empowered followers to be innovative and to use their initiative, creativity and imagination to complete tasks. It requires a great deal of trust on the part of the leader and the willingness to allow followers to fail. Jesus illustrated this concept in the well-known parable of the minas, as recorded in the 19th chapter of Luke.

> "A certain nobleman went into a far country to receive for himself a kingdom and to return. So he called ten of his servants, delivered to them ten minas, and said to them, *'Do business till I come'*" (Luke 19:12, 13 *emphasis added*).

The parable continues with the nobleman returning to praise his servants who have invested wisely and to condemn the one servant who did not earn any interest on his investment. He did not leave them with instructions on *how* to invest his money, he simply said, "Do business." This is true empowerment:

- each servant was given *responsibility* for a sum of

money
- each had the *authority* to invest the money as they determined best
- each was held *accountable* for the return they achieved on the investment

How do you empower your followers? Do you use mission-type orders? Have you made yourself available to critique them as they complete initial assignments being careful to offer praise along with constructive criticism? Have you chosen small assignments with a good probability for success for these future leaders or do they perceive each challenge as a "do or die" situation? Have you shown them by example how to faithfully complete an assignment using the principles and precepts you have taught them?

Phase V: Deployment

The final phase of Jesus' strategy was to *deploy* his followers. He turned over leadership to them and they would now assume responsibility for the ministry. He had arrived at this point in His work by:
- preparing Himself to lead
- picking potential leaders who would succeed Him
- enabling them
- empowering them
- now, He would deploy them.

His orders were strategic, mission-type orders from a macro-perspective. They had a broad sweep extending well beyond the limited human perspective of His followers. Jesus had never traveled more than a few miles from the place He was born and raised. His family's flight to Egypt as a child was the farthest He had been from home yet His vision was global (see Matthew 2:13-15).

He emphasized the disciples' mission and His vision for the ministry three times. The first occasion was the night before His betrayal and arrest. He began by reminding them of their first trial when He sent them out in pairs,

> And He said to them, "When I sent you without money bag, knapsack, and sandals, did you lack anything?" So they said, "Nothing." Then he said to them, "But now, he who has a money bag, let him take it, and likewise a knapsack; and he who has no sword, let him sell his garment and buy one. For I say to you that this which is written must still be accomplished in Me" (Luke 22:35-37).

They had gone and ministered only to the Jews, but now He sent them out to the entire world! They would be on their own and He knew that they would experience severe resistance and even persecution. He reassured them that they were well prepared and able to accomplish the aims of His ministry.

The second occasion was following Jesus' death on a cross when He first appeared to his eleven disciples and gave them "the Great Commission."

> And Jesus came and spoke to them, saying, "All authority has been given to Me in heaven and on earth. Go therefore and make disciples of all the nations, baptizing them in the name of the Father and of the Son and of the Holy Spirit, teaching them to observe all things that I have commanded you; and lo, I am with you always, even to the end of the age" (Matthew 28:18-20).

Again, we see in this statement the three elements necessary for true empowerment:

- Responsibility: "go ... and make disciples ... baptizing them ... (and) teaching them"
- Authority: "All authority has been given to me" and I am giving you that same authority
- Accountability: "I am with you always" to encourage you and hold you accountable

The night before His arrest, Jesus had assured his followers that He would "not leave you orphans; I will come to you" (John 14:18). And He had assured them that they could count on His continual support in the work that He was sending them out to accomplish. He had told them that after His death, God would send them "another Helper":

> "But the Helper, the Holy Spirit, whom the
> Father will send in My name, He will teach
> you all things, and bring to your remembrance
> all things that I said to you" (John 14:26).

The third and final time was at the end of His forty days on earth following His resurrection. He had told His disciples to remain in Jerusalem for the "Promise of the Father" when they would be baptized with the Holy Spirit. They had asked Him if this was now the time when He would drive out the Romans and restore the kingdom of Israel and He replied,

> "It is not for you to know times or seasons
> which the Father has put in His own author-
> ity. But you shall receive power when the
> Holy Spirit has come upon you; and you
> shall be witnesses to Me in Jerusalem, and in
> all Judea and Samaria, and to the end of the

earth" (Acts 1:7, 8).

Again, Jesus specified the limit of their authority (i.e., they would not know the exact timing of future events), but He reaffirmed their global mission and assured them of His continual support.

And so Jesus deploys the new leaders of His ministry with a three-part order:

- Make disciples, baptize, and teach them (their mission)
- Go to all nations (their market)
- He would support them (through the Holy Spirit)

Jesus stepped away from active leadership of His ministry with a mission-type order that specified purpose and scope but left the methods and means up to the disciples. He assured them that they were capable of assuming leadership but that they could always count on His guidance and encouragement.

This five-phase model is appropriate for many types of organizations. A leader must first *prepare* himself to lead through education, training and experience. As we have seen, a servant leader is *called* to lead. He prepares himself for leadership but waits for a calling to assume a leadership role. He carefully *picks* his closest subordinates with the potential to become servant leaders themselves. He systematically *enables* them to assume leadership roles by providing them with the tools they will need, and especially by his personal example. He *empowers* them by delegating responsibility, authority, and accountability, first with small trials, and then with progressively greater tasks. When they have demonstrated competence to assume responsibility, he *turns over* leadership to his subordinates using mission-type orders being careful to state the purpose but not the means for accomplishing the goals.

The final phase of this model does not mean that leaders

must completely cut themselves off from any decision-making responsibility once they have reached this point. That will be the case, of course, when the leader retires or moves on to another job. But in those cases where the leader remains with the organization it simply means that his subordinates are doing most of the day-to-day decision-making. This frees him to plan, to strategize, to innovate, and to seek out new markets and new products. It provides him time to *think*! In any organization, there are very few decisions that the top leader needs to make. This model frees the chief executive from making decisions that others, properly prepared and trained, are capable of making and allows him time to do those important things that only he can do.

In the next chapter we will examine the personal characteristics of Jesus as He lived out His model for leadership.

Endnote

[2] talmid (pl. talmidim): A disciple or student of a rabbi whose desire was not only to know what his teacher knew but also to become like him. (Laan 1996)

11

Jesus Wept

Meekness is submissive power under perfect control.
—Anonymous

In Chapter 2, we examined trait theories and discovered that this approach to leadership research had been largely overtaken by other research methods due to its failure to consistently predict successful leaders. However, we also learned that recent studies have suggested that there are some distinguishing traits that seem to set leaders apart, including intelligence and assertiveness. A new study concluded that there was an identifiable set of traits required for future public leaders.

Greenleaf argues that servant leaders do have an identifiable set of traits, as discussed in Chapter 6, namely: initiative, intelligence, foresight, and perception. Likewise, George Barna contends that Christian leaders have a distinguishing set of traits that set them apart from their followers and other leaders (see Chapter 8).

Jesus' Leadership Traits

Jesus displayed six unique traits as a leader that warrant our attention. Traits, by their very nature, were considered to be God-given characteristics; i.e., you were born with them. However, few would argue with the notion that one can acquire certain traits through deliberate effort such as becoming more compassionate towards others or more trustworthy. Most would agree that a child raised in a family where prejudice is preached and practiced could overcome that early prejudicial thinking through prayer and practice. Therefore, the leadership traits of Jesus may be learned and put into practice by each of us.

The six traits are: *compassion, humility, impartiality, integrity, trustworthiness,* and *wisdom.* Let's look at these traits and see how Jesus applied them in leading His followers.

Compassion. Jesus displayed compassion toward all He met and in a variety of situations including at a friend's wedding, at an only son's funeral, toward a wealthy young seeker, at the death of a friend, and for all who were sick in body, soul or spirit. He would regularly allow interruptions to His plans to minister to someone in need without appearing perturbed or distracted. When He turned His attention to the person in need, He focused His entire being upon that person. The one healed knew that for that moment in time they had Jesus' complete and full attention.

> *The LORD is gracious and full of compassion,*
> *Slow to anger and great in mercy.*
> *The LORD is good to all,*
> *And His tender mercies are over all His works.*
>
> —Psalm 145:8, 9

Jesus and His mother, along with His disciples, had been invited to the wedding of a family friend in Cana of Galilee, a few miles from their home in Capernaum. A Jewish wedding was a joyous time of celebration and pride for the families of the bride and groom and everyone had worked diligently to make sure this wedding was a success. Midway through the gala reception a stir began to run through the crowd, "They have run out of wine!" When His mother heard this, she immediately informed Jesus of this embarrassing development. What a disgrace this would be! Everyone will forget about the beauty of the bride and the lovely flower arrangements and only remember that they ran out of wine at the reception! Jesus was well aware of His timing and He knew that this was not really the time or the place to begin performing miracles. But He had compassion for the family of the bride and their likely shame caused by this situation. Rescuing the day, He changed six large masonry containers of water into the finest wine (see John 2:1-11).

Jesus displayed the most human of emotions, compassion over the death of a loved one. Having been informed of the sickness of His good friend Lazarus, Jesus delayed returning to Bethany because His plans for His friend had a strategic purpose beyond simply raising him from death. However, when He came to the tomb where they had laid Lazarus' body, "Jesus wept. Then the Jews said, 'See how He loved him!'" (John 11:35, 36). Jesus knew that He would raise Lazarus from the dead but He was still overcome with emotion by the thought of His friend lying stone cold in a dark tomb. He did not make an effort to hide His emotion from His disciples. Real men do cry!

He was always compassionate toward those least able in society to care for themselves, the poor, the sick, widows and orphans. As He was approaching the city of Nain, He was met by a burial procession coming out of the city. Held aloft was the body of a young man, the only son of a widow. Knowing that the woman's only means of support lay dead on that burial pallet, Jesus "had compassion on her and said to her, 'Do not weep.'"

> Then He came and touched the open coffin,
> and those who carried him stood still. And
> He said, "Young man, I say to you, arise."
> So he who was dead sat up and began to
> speak. And He presented him to his mother.
> (Luke 7:13-15).

His compassion knew no class, color, or cultural barriers. Once, He encountered a young man from the ruling class who was seeking the way to salvation and eternal life. Jesus knew in His spirit that the only stumbling block between this man and the kingdom of God was his wealth. The man's possessions had become his god. Knowing this, Jesus,

looking at him, loved him, and said to him,
"One thing you lack: Go your way, sell whatever you have and give to the poor, and you
will have treasure in heaven; and come, take
up the cross, and follow Me" (Mark 10:21).

His "disciples were astonished at His words" since they
believed that the rich were most blessed by God; why just
look at all they have! Jesus went on to explain how "hard it
is for those who trust in riches to enter the kingdom of
God!" (Mark 10:24) Jesus meant that the temptations of
wealth are so great that they can easily draw a person away
from the kingdom of God.

> *"But many who are first will be last,
> and the last first."*
> —*Matthew 19:30*

The Gospels are filled with examples of Jesus showing
compassion on all those who were sick regardless of their
station in life:

- He went about Galilee "healing all kinds of sickness
  and all kinds of disease among the people" (Matthew
  4:23).
- A leper came and worshiped Him saying, "Lord, if
  You are willing, You can make me clean." Jesus,
  "moved with compassion, stretched out His hand and
  touched him, and said to him, "I am willing; be
  cleansed" (Mark 4:41).
- A Roman Centurion came to Him and pleaded for
  healing for his servant and Jesus healed him because
  of the faithfulness of his master (Matthew 8:5-13).
- He saw Peter's mother-in-law sick with a fever and

healed her (Matthew 8:14, 15).
- One of the members of the Jewish ruling party pleaded with Him to restore life to his daughter who had just died. He immediately went and raised her to life (Matthew 9:18-25).
- The blind called out to Him and He "had compassion and touched their eyes. And immediately their eyes received sight" (Matthew 9:27-30, and 20:34).
- He cast out a demon from a mute man who immediately spoke (Matthew 9:32, 33).
- While teaching in the cities, "... when He saw the multitudes, He was moved with compassion for them, because they were weary and scattered, like sheep having no shepherd" (Matthew 9:36).
- "He was moved with compassion for them, and healed their sick," just prior to feeding five thousand with five loaves of bread and two fish (Matthew 14:14).
- Again, He feeds another large crowd who have come to Him for teaching and healing: "Now Jesus called His disciples to Himself and said, 'I have compassion on the multitude, because they have now continued with Me three days and have nothing to eat. And I do not want to send them away hungry, lest they faint on the way'" (Matthew 15:32).

> *For I was hungry and you gave me something to eat, I was thirsty and you gave me something to drink, I was a stranger and you invited me in, I needed clothes and you clothed me, I was sick and you looked after me, I was in prison and you came to visit me.*
> *—Matthew 25:35, 36*

In the lives of great leaders, one of the characteristics that appears common to many is the presence of adversity, often at an early age. This adversity may be physical (sickness, stature, handicap, etc.), social or economic status, or parental abandonment (emotional or physical). What sets great leaders apart from the rest of society is their reaction to adversity: they overcome it! By struggling through adversity, many leaders grow in compassion, character, and understanding that those without this same experience never develop.

Jesus was compassionate, in part, due to the adversity in His life. He was raised in Nazareth, a town apparently despised by many Jews. When Philip, Jesus' newest disciple and a native of Bethsaida, told Nathanael about Him, Nathanael responded, "Nazareth! Can anything good come from there?" (John 1:46). As a child, Jesus knew that He was special and the scriptures tell us he remained sinless. This, of itself, would have set Jesus apart from the rest of the boys His age. "Come on, Jesus, are you a sissy?" was probably a taunt He heard often.

But the hardest thing for young Jesus to cope with must have been growing up with the vicious whispers that His was an out-of-wedlock birth. I doubt that His mother Mary ever quite overcame the back-alley gossips and pointed-fingers-behind-her-back of the "best" women of Nazareth as they passed judgment on this young virgin girl impregnated—so she said—by the Holy Spirit. Jesus would have endured the crushing boyhood taunts of his classmates that have destroyed many a young spirit.

The charge of illegitimacy followed Jesus into manhood, as we see in this exchange between Jesus and the Pharisees as recorded in the Gospel of John. Jesus had just told the Pharisees that if they remained slaves to sin they were following the example of Satan.

Then they said to Him, "We were not born of
fornication; we have one Father—God"
(John 8:41).

The Pharisees brought up an old charge that had
followed Jesus all of His life: that He was illegitimate. As
an adult, He was called a half-breed, demon-possessed, a
drunk, a friend of sinners, but this label hung on a young
boy was devastating. Jesus had to develop mental toughness
early in life while developing a special sensitivity to the
needs of those whom society looked down upon. He understood well Paul's encouraging words to the Romans,

> Not only so, but we also rejoice in our suffer-
> ings, because we know that suffering
> produces perseverance; perseverance, charac-
> ter; and character, hope (Romans 5:3, 4 NIV).

Humility. Jesus reflected the humility expected of lead-
ers going back to at least the time of Moses (c. 1400 B.C.).
He was aware of God's instructions to the future leaders of
Israel that they should not expect or accept any special priv-
ileges not afforded to everyone else. Moses instructed
Israel's kings to make a personal copy of this law

> and it shall be with him, and he shall read it
> all the days of his life, that he may learn to
> fear the LORD his God and be careful to
> observe all the words of this law and these
> statutes, that his heart may not be lifted
> above his brethren (Deuteronomy 17:19, 20).

A quick review of the history of the kings of Israel will
reveal that many of them did not adhere to this law; but
Jesus said He did not come to abolish the law but to fulfill

it. He lived out the law the way God intended it. Jesus never claimed greatness for Himself but always reflected God's glory by saying, "I can of myself do nothing" but only what my Father tells me (John 5:30).

Several times He hid from those who would make Him king. As He entered Jerusalem for that fatal, last time, crowds began to line the road leading up to the city. Men and women jostled for the front row hoping for a glimpse of the prophet from Galilee who they hoped would throw out the Romans and restore the Jewish homeland. "Have you heard? Jesus of Nazareth is coming to save us! The Son of David will be our deliverer! They say He is the long-awaited Messiah!" Many in that boisterous crowd must have wondered why their savior was not riding a great white charger as did the conquering heroes of Rome. But this was to fulfill the prophecy of Zechariah that the promised Messiah would enter Jerusalem,

> Lowly and riding on a donkey,
> A colt, the foal of a donkey (Zechariah 9:9).

As with many people today, His disciples found it diffi-cult to understand the concept of servant as leader. The leaders they saw among their own people, or among the Romans, were set apart and expected special treatment. Jesus would often use children to illustrate the type of unpretentious attitude that His disciples should emulate. Once they came to Him asking who would be the greatest in the kingdom of heaven and he called a child and set him in their midst and said,

> "Assuredly, I say to you, unless you are converted and become as little children, you will by no means enter the kingdom of heaven. Therefore, whoever humbles

himself as this little child is the greatest in
the kingdom of heaven" (Matthew 18:3, 4).

In Jesus' time leprosy was incurable and thought to be
transmitted by touch. Therefore, lepers were shunned to
the outskirts of towns and forced to cry out "Unclean,
unclean" whenever anyone approached them. Knowing
this, Jesus, the respected rabbi, accepted a dinner invitation to a leper's house and let the tongues wag (Matthew
26:6)! He was making a statement that He did not consider
the leper unclean and yes, even he could enter the kingdom of heaven.

> *"Humility must always be the portion
> of any man who receives acclaim
> earned in the blood of his followers
> and the sacrifice of his friends."*
> —Dwight David Eisenhower

He would often criticize the Pharisees for demanding
special privileges and instructed His disciples to not follow
their example:

> "When you are invited by anyone to a
> wedding feast, do not sit down in the best
> place, lest one more honorable than you be
> invited by him ... but go and sit down in the
> lowest place, so that when he who invited
> you comes he may say to you, 'Friend, go up
> higher.' For whoever exalts himself will be
> humbled, and he who humbles himself will
> be exalted" (Luke 14:8-14).

Jesus commanded His disciples to simply do their duty without expecting anything in return while holding Himself to that same standard:

> "So likewise you, when you have done all those things which you are commanded, say 'We are unprofitable servants. We have done what was our duty to do'" (Luke 17:10).

Near the end of His three-year ministry, Jesus ate supper with His disciples for the last time. He had taught them time and again that they were to be as servants to one another. He said not to be like the scribes and the Pharisees for "all their works they do to be seen by men" (Matthew 23:5). He contrasted their behavior with the Roman leaders:

> "The kings of the Gentiles exercise lordship over them, and those who exercise authority over them are called 'benefactors.' But not so among you; on the contrary, he who is greatest among you, let him be as the younger, and he who governs as he who serves" (Luke 22:25, 26).

He had likened this to becoming like an innocent child and yet they still didn't get it! He had told them three times what would happen to Him, their leader and Lord, when they would go up to Jerusalem: that He would be falsely accused by the Jewish leaders and dragged before a kangaroo court; He would be beaten and handed over to the Romans; they would mock and flog Him and then lead Him out of the city and crucify Him. And how did the disciples react? They continued to argue who among them would be the greatest! I can just see Jesus shaking His head in disbelief. Why can't they understand!

As a final, unforgettable illustration, Jesus rose after supper and took off his outer garments. He poured water into a bowl and wrapped a towel around His waist. The disciples must have watched this with fascination. What was Jesus doing now? He was always doing things we don't understand but what does this mean? Surely He's not going to wash our feet! That is the job of the lowliest servant in the house. Surely the Master would not stoop to this! But stoop He did and proceeded to wash the disciples feet. When He had finished, He sat down and said,

> "Do you know what I have done to you? You call Me Teacher and Lord, and you say well, for so I am. If I then, your Lord and Teacher, have washed your feet, you also ought to wash one another's feet. For *I have given you an example* that you should do as I have done to you" (John 13:12-15 *emphasis added*).

These were radical words to a class-conscious culture and they are just as radical today. Jesus was speaking to the attitude of the heart. His disciples had grown up in a culture where wealth and position expected privilege and praise. This was a society where God blessed some with health and wealth while others were cursed and doomed to a short, miserable life of poverty and sickness, or so they believed. Jesus explained in a way they would never forget that every person has equal worth in the eyes of God. And that they, as His future leaders, must develop a sense of humility and impartiality toward others that was completely opposite to the world's values. His was truly an upside-down kingdom.

> *Another time, someone asked Mother*
> *(Teresa), "What will you do when you*
> *are no longer Mother General?"*
> *Mother thought about this for a second*
> *and said with a smile, "I am good at*
> *cleaning toilets, you know!"*
> — *from Collopy (1996)*

We have evidence that this time the disciples did learn their lesson. George Hunter explains in *The Celtic Way of Evangelism* (2000) that in the monastic communities established by Patrick in the fifth century, hospitality played an important role in the evangelism of pre-Christian people. A visitor to one of these communities would be welcomed by the abbot with "all courtesy of love." After gently inquiring about

> what had prompted your visit (and so begin
> the ministry of conversation), and he would
> read a scripture for you, offer a prayer for you,
> and extend the "kiss of peace." The abbot
> would *wash your feet* (from your journey by
> foot), and would show you to the guest house"
> (Hunter 2000, 52, *emphasis added*).

12

Unto the Least of These

*Do not think of yourself more highly than you ought ... so,
in Christ we who are many form one body, and each
member belongs to all the others ... If a man's gift ... is
leadership, let him govern diligently.*
—*Romans 12:3-8*

In the last chapter, we examined Jesus' leadership traits of
compassion and humility. In this chapter we will explore
His four other traits: *impartiality, integrity, trustworthiness,
and wisdom.*

Impartiality. Jesus only saw what people *could be* not
what they were. His message was one of radical impartiality
to all classes of society. He shocked the Jewish leaders of
His day by granting women and slaves equality with free
men. He said He had come for the powerless ones of society
rather than the powerful. Jesus used a well-known parable
to illustrate this principle.

In response to a lawyer's question, "And who is my

neighbor?" (Luke 10:29), Jesus answered with the parable of the Good Samaritan. The irony, certainly not lost on His audience, was that the hero of the story was not the priest or the Levite, but the Samaritan. Samaritans were a people of mixed heritage who lived between Galilee and Judea. Eight hundred years earlier, the king of Assyria had forcibly replaced the Israelites with people from Babylon and beyond and they took possession of the cities of Samaria. These Gentiles intermarried with the Jews and worshiped the Jewish God but continued to practice their former pagan rituals (2 Kings 17:24-41). The Jews universally denigrated them. To suggest that only one of these people knew the true meaning of brotherly love certainly must have shocked the hearers of this parable.

And then Jesus said that He had come to break the "Jews only" covenant (or so they believed) that God had with His people. However, He made it clear that He understood that His mission was first to the Jews and then to the Gentiles. One of Paul's "mysteries," described in his epistles, was that the Messiah had come for both Jew and Gentile.

Jesus was on the Mediterranean shore when a Canaanite woman approached Him begging Him to heal her demon-possessed daughter.

> But He answered and said, "I was not sent except to the lost sheep of the house of Israel." Then she came and worshiped Him, saying, "Lord, help me!" But He answered and said, "It is not good to take the children's bread and throw it to the little dogs." And she said, "Yes, Lord, yet even the little dogs eat the crumbs which fall from their masters' table" (Matthew 15:24-27).

Overwhelmed by her demonstration of faith, Jesus healed her daughter. Although He knew that His mission was to be first fully revealed to the House of Israel, He confirmed that faith was the discriminator, not heritage.

> *"What a shock it was to discover that greatness comes through servanthood, and leadership through becoming a slave of all."*
> —J. Oswald Sanders

In Jesus' day (and to many still today) wealth was equated with God's favor. How could a person achieve riches and power without God's blessing? Conversely, the poor and sick were believed to be cursed for sins they had committed or perhaps for the sins of their fathers. Jesus used the parable of the workers in the vineyard to explain God's unmerited love and grace to everyone whom He has chosen regardless of their worthiness.

Early in the morning, a landowner went to the local union hall and hired laborers for his vineyard. He agreed to pay them the standard daily wage and they set to work. He hired more workers three hours later and put them to work, too. At noon, he hired more workers and again an hour before quitting time. At the end of the day, the men lined up for their pay. When the landowner entered the room, he ordered the workers hired last to the front of the line. These were paid a full-day's wages and left with smiles on their faces. When the men who had worked the entire day moved to the paymaster they expected to be paid more but they likewise received only the standard wage.

"And when they received it, they complained against the landowner, saying, 'These last men have worked only one hour, and you made them equal to us who have borne the burden and the heat of the day.' But he answered one of them and said, 'Friend, I am doing you no wrong. Did you not agree with me for a denarius? Take what is yours and go your way. I wish to give to this last man the same as to you. Is it not lawful for me to do what I wish with my own things? Or is your eye evil because I am good?' "So the last will be first, and the first last. For many are called, but few are chosen" (Matthew 20:1-16).

Jesus does not favor those with special talent over those less capable. He does expect each one to do his best according to his ability. He does not accept mediocrity. This is illustrated with the parable of the talents.

A man was to be away from his business for an extended period of time. Rather than leave his money idle, he entrusted discretionary funds to each of three top lieutenants. However, they each did not receive the same amount. One received $5,000, one $2,000, and the third received only $1,000. This disbursement was based on the businessman's assessment of their abilities. When he returned, the man found that indeed his most gifted aide had invested wisely and had doubled his money. Likewise, the second aide had also doubled his money. However, the third man had merely hidden his $1,000 for fear of losing it and so returned to him the original investment. After praising equally his first two aides for using his funds wisely, the businessman turned to the third man:

"Then he who had received the one talent came and said, 'Lord, I knew you to be a hard man, reaping where you have not sown, and gathering where you have not scattered seed. And I was afraid, and went and hid your talent in the ground. Look, there you have what is yours.' But his lord answered and said to him, 'You wicked and lazy servant, you knew that I reap where I have not sown, and gather where I have not scattered seed. So you ought to have deposited my money with the bankers, and at my coming I would have received back my own with interest. Therefore take the talent from him, and give it to him who has ten talents. For to everyone who has, more will be given, and he will have abundance; but from him who does not have, even what he has will be taken away" (Matthew 25:14-29).

Notice that the businessman did not discriminate against the subordinate who returned only $4,000 while another returned $10,000 since each had doubled the funds entrusted to him according to his ability. Only the third man who had not used his ability to its fullest received the condemnation of his superior. "Good enough" is not good enough for Jesus!

Finally, Jesus instructs His disciples that at His Second

Coming He will judge all men by their treatment of His "brothers," the downcast in society:

> "Then the King will say to those on His right hand, 'Come, you blessed of My Father, inherit the kingdom prepared for you from the foundation of the world; for I was hungry and you gave Me food; I was thirsty and you gave Me drink; I was a stranger and you took Me in; I was naked and you clothed Me; I was sick and you visited Me; I was in prison and you came to Me. Assuredly, I say to you, inasmuch as you did it to one of the least of these My brethren, you did it to Me" (Matthew 25:34-40).

Integrity. Webster's Dictionary defines integrity as the characteristic of moral soundness, honesty, and uprightness. Is integrity an important trait for leaders? Yes, integrity is vital since leadership is the unconscious expression of the character and personality of the leader (Puryear, 1971, 289). And, the organization, often unconsciously, takes on the character and values of its leader. A recent study suggests that integrity is critical to leadership of public organizations (see chapter 2).

Jesus certainly taught that integrity was a key ingredient to successful leadership. The righteous man, Job, who endured faithfully through testing and trials that would fell a lesser man, is a model of integrity: "Till I die I will not put away my integrity from me" (Job 27:5b). King David acknowledged that God seeks men of integrity: "I know, my God, that you test the heart and are pleased with integrity" (1 Chronicles 29:17 NIV).

Integrity marks the character of a leader and those lacking this important trait will eventually be exposed.

In the Marine Corps it was known as a crime involving moral turpitude; i.e., a breach of integrity.

A senior staff officer had sought my counsel regarding one of his staff non-commissioned officers (SNCOs) whose name appeared on the promotion list for gunnery sergeant (E-7). At issue was the fact that this man had been court-martialed a few years before. The staff sergeant had been convicted of filing a fraudulent travel claim for several thousand dollars. Now he had been selected for advancement and his boss questioned whether we should allow the promotion to take place.

Normally, this would not be an issue for me as the installation commander. SNCOs were selected for promotion by a board convened in Washington based on their time-in-grade and their performance record. Those selected for promotion were advanced over a period of several months as vacancies occurred unless a commander in the chain of command objected. I asked my senior attorney to review the case and give me an opinion as to whether I should make an exception in this case. Her research showed that the staff sergeant had been found guilty and was fined but had not been reduced in grade. This was unusual, as normally a crime of this nature would dictate at least a one-grade reduction. I asked her to check with the judge in that case to determine, if possible, the rationale behind the lenient sentence. The judge's reply was surprising.

The Marine in question was an E-6 at the time of his court-martial and had been selected for promotion. The judge determined that by awarded him a reduction in grade to E-5, he would in effect be giving him a two-grade reduction since the defendant would soon be promoted to E-7. Instead, he had his name removed from the promotion list thereby effectively "busting" him one grade. With that mystery solved, I convened my senior staff and asked for their counsel. To a man, including the Sergeant-Major, the senior enlisted Marine on the station, they all recommended allowing the promotion to go forward, saying, in effect, "He's paid his dues; go ahead and promote him." I still had reservations so I called my boss, the commanding general. He had apparently already been alerted to the case as he advised me that I had no choice but to promote the man in question.

I still had serious reservations since the man's crime involved a breach of integrity: he had lied for his personal monetary gain. What would be the reaction of the other staff sergeants who did not have a courts-martial conviction and had not been selected for promotion if I allowed this to go forward, I wondered? I prayed about my decision and determined, in spite of counsel otherwise, to object to the promotion.

I called the staff sergeant to my office and informed him that I would not promote him. I explained to him that integrity was essential to leaders and that he had demonstrated a serious breach of integrity. Needles to say, he was not happy and vowed to appeal my decision.

Two weeks later, as his appeal was working its way up the chain of command, the senior judge advocate ran into my office, "Guess who just got caught shoplifting at the Parris Island Exchange?" she asked. "Our staff sergeant!" Shortly thereafter, I heard from the lawyers at headquarters who sided with my decision. Of course by that time, he had sealed his own fate and was asked to seek employment elsewhere.

Jesus had the reputation as a man of integrity. The Pharisees were laying plans to trap Jesus into saying something that could be considered heretical or treasonous and thereby bring charges against Him. Inciting rebellion against Caesar was punishable by death therefore they tried to trick Him into speaking against their Roman conquerors:

> "Teacher," they said, "we know you are a man of integrity and that you teach the way of God in accordance with the truth. You aren't swayed by men because you pay no attention to who they are. Tell us then, what is your opinion? Is it right to pay taxes to Caesar or not?" (Matthew 22:16, 17 NIV).

Jesus demonstrated His integrity by asking for a coin and then instructing His inquisitors to pay taxes to the one whose face appeared on the coin. He had distinguished Himself as a man of integrity because He would not equivocate His teaching of God's law to please the rich and powerful or to win favor with a few. The truth was the truth regardless of the audience. Even the Pharisees had to grudgingly admit that this was unlike many teachers of His day.

A person of integrity speaks the truth in love.

A person with integrity keeps his word even when it seems unfair and it involves personal sacrifice.

> In our era of easy credit, crushing debt loads, and a record number of personal bankruptcies, David was an exception. A young building contractor in Maine, he enjoyed a growing successful partnership. For several years during the booming 1990's, he and his partner struggled to keep up with the demand for new houses. Then the bottom fell out. As mortgage rates crept upward, the demand for vacation and second homes rapidly fell off. Eventually, David could no longer service the debt his business had accumulated and he was forced to file for bankruptcy protection. The difference between David's story and so many others like him was that he was determined to pay back all the money he owed— and not just 10 cents on the dollar. While his partner walked out, David continued to pay back his creditors through a new fertilizer-from-the-sea business venture. His integrity and commitment so impressed the local banks that they hired him to serve as a consultant for new construction loan proposals. He is still paying off his partner's bill to a local dentist.

Trustworthiness. An important corollary to integrity is trustworthiness. Earlier we examined the fundamental requirement for a leader to develop trust among his followers. He does this by first being *trustworthy*. A person of integrity is one who can be trusted. He is true to his word. He does not have a second, unseen agenda—one of self-promotion. He is open and shares information freely with his followers. He is not afraid of communicating bad news along with the good. At the root of most failed or failing organizations is a *lack of trust*: in the leader, in each other, or in the "system."

I had been teaching at a small Christian college for three years when one Saturday morning as I was working in my garden, I received an urgent call from the college president. Could I come and see him on an important matter? When I arrived at his office about an hour later, he told me that the director of athletics had just resigned and would I take on that responsibility while he looked for a full-time replacement? Although it was very near the end of the semester with me teaching a full load and final exams looming, I agreed to give it a try. I did this primarily because I was aware of some of the problems in the athletic department and I knew how important inter-collegiate athletics was to the students and the entire college.

My assessment of the culture of the athletic department was pretty grim. Lack of trust, brought about by fear, permeated the staff. I learned that coaches would enter side doors of their building so as to avoid passing the athletic director's office in route to their own offices. There they would hide until they had to come out for a practice or a class. There was little dialogue between staff members and meetings were infrequent. What meetings were held were largely unproductive as each staff member worked to protect his or her own turf from being exploited by another. Little information was made available to the coaching staff including their own budgets. Although I believe the former athletic director meant well, he retained all authority. Since he also coached a sport, other coaches believed he favored his own sport with the lion's share of the athletic budget. The athletic staff felt isolated from the rest of the campus emotionally and physically. The athletic director had the only computer and none of the staff had access to the college network or email. Coaches generally did not feel like a part of the faculty and did not participate in faculty meetings. Retention was low and coaches frequently stayed only a year or two before moving on.

Considering all of that, where do you begin?

I diagnosed the root problem as lack of *trust*. It began at the top. The former athletic director apparently did not trust his boss or his staff. His staff, in turn, did not trust him. They believed (incorrectly, I was to find out) that the administration did not care about them so they did not trust the senior leadership. This was where I had to begin. Our first meeting was one I will not forget: I'd called the entire staff to meet in the athletic training room. I opened with prayer and asked each person to grab the hand of the person next to him. It was as if they were reaching out to one another for the first time. I believe those first few minutes of heart-felt prayer broke through the wall of mistrust that surrounded that organization. Over the next few weeks, I began delegating authority and accountability along with responsibility to the staff. Our biweekly meetings began with a devotion led by a staff member and we would spend time praying for each other's needs. I was deliberately open with them about their budgets so that each one knew not only what their budget was but also everyone else's. With a lot of support from the administration, each coach received a laptop computer and was soon connected to the college network and email system. They were granted faculty rank and encouraged to participate in faculty events. They began to feel like they were partners in the campus community rather than strangers. They began to trust as they saw that their leaders were trustworthy.

In the three years Jesus had lived with His disciples, they had come to see Him as trustworthy and He lived out that trust. After cleaning out the temple of the moneychangers, Jesus used a withered fig tree to illustrate His trustworthiness. The disciples were astonished that the tree that Jesus had cursed had dried up:

> So Jesus answered and said to them, "Have faith in God. For assuredly, I say to you, whoever says to this mountain, 'Be removed and be cast into the sea,' and does not doubt in his heart, but believes that those things he says will be done, he will have whatever he says. Therefore I say to you, whatever things

you ask when you pray, believe that you
receive them, and you will have them"
(Mark 11:22-24).

During His last meal with His followers, Jesus once
again told them that soon He was going to be put to death
but that they should not be anxious. They could trust Him
and all that He had taught them about the kingdom of God.

"Let not your heart be troubled; you believe
in God, believe also in Me. In My Father's
house are many mansions; if it were not so, I
would have told you. I go to prepare a place
for you. And if I go and prepare a place for
you, I will come again and receive you to
Myself; that where I am, there you may be
also" (John 14:1-3).

Thomas responded to Jesus' next statement, "And
where I go you know, and the way you know," by saying,
"Lord, we do not know where You are going, and how can
we know the way?" (John 14:4, 5). Jesus answered him by
claiming to be the source of all truth:

Jesus said to him, "I am the way, the truth,
and the life. No one comes to the Father
except through Me" (John 14:6).

That extraordinary statement was followed by His
unequivocal claim of divinity: "He who has seen Me has
seen the Father" (John 14:9b). Then He assured them that
they could trust Him to always support them in their work:

"Most assuredly, I say to you, he who
believes in Me, the works that I do he will do

also; and greater works then these he will do,
because I go to My Father. And whatever you
ask in My name, that I will do, that the Father
may be glorified in the Son. If you ask
anything in My name, I will do it" (John
14:12-14).

Knowing that they were still fearful of what the future
would bring, He assured them that God the Father would
send them "another Helper," the "Spirit of truth" who would
live within them to encourage and uphold them (John 14:16,
17). His assurance that, "I will not leave you orphans; I will
come to you," fell on receptive ears.

Following His crucifixion and burial, some of the
women came to prepare Jesus' body according to the Jewish
custom. They found the stone rolled from the entrance to the
tomb and the burial chamber empty. Entering the tomb, they
saw an angel sitting where the body should have been. The
angel assured them that Jesus had risen, just as He had told
His disciples,

"But go tell his disciples and Peter, 'He is
going ahead of you into Galilee. There you
will see him, just as he told you'" (Mark 16:7
NIV).

And they did.

Wisdom. Wisdom is more than intelligence. Webster's
defines wisdom as the ability to judge soundly and deal saga-
ciously with facts, especially as they relate to life and
conduct; discernment and judgment; discretion; sagacity. In
other words, wisdom is the *application* of knowledge and
experience to life. As we saw in chapter 2, some early studies
of leader's traits concluded that intelligence was a dominant

trait. Greenleaf argues for intelligence as a required trait for leaders but his meaning clearly relates more to wisdom than knowing facts as he stresses the ability to apply intuition to the decision process.

Jesus would continually confound the leading teachers of His day with His wisdom yet He was not formally trained, as was His disciple Paul. Certainly, He knew the scriptures well but He had an understanding of the meaning of the laws and prophecies that often astounded the wise men of His day. We do not know much about the early life of Jesus from the scriptures yet the information we do have suggests that He was recognized as having great wisdom from an early age. Luke's one sentence description of Jesus' life between the ages of two months and twelve years suggests this:

> And the Child grew and became strong in spirit, filled with wisdom; and the grace of God was upon Him (Luke 2:40).

When He was twelve years old, His parents went up to Jerusalem, as they did annually, for the Feast of the Passover. As they were returning home, they discovered that Jesus was not with the company of relatives and friends. Immediately, they returned to Jerusalem and found Him in the temple,

> sitting in the midst of the teachers, both listening to them and asking them questions. And all who heard Him were astonished at His understanding and answers (Luke 2:46).

When Jesus announced the start of His public ministry in His hometown synagogue, many were astonished that this local man had such understanding:

> And when the Sabbath had come, He began
> to teach in the synagogue. And many hearing
> Him were astonished, saying, "Where did
> this Man get these things? And what wisdom
> is this which is given to Him, that such
> mighty works are performed by His hands!
> Is this not the carpenter, the Son of Mary,
> and brother of James, Joses, Judas, and
> Simon? (Mark 6:2, 3).

Believers and non-believers alike universally recognize Jesus as being exceptionally wise. Gandhi, a modern proponent of servant leadership, was not a Christian yet he studied the life and teachings of Jesus. Jesus would often conclude a teaching with the challenge, "He who has ears to hear, let him hear!", meaning, those with wisdom will apply this lesson to their lives.

The experts in the law would often question Jesus about the application of Jewish law to daily living hoping to trip Him up and thereby have a punishable offense with which to charge Him. Examples included whether it was lawful to pay taxes to Caesar (Matthew 22:15-21), and the proper punishment for a woman caught in adultery (John 8:3-11). He responded to those who accused Him of being a glutton and heavy drinker by pointing to His miraculous works, "But wisdom is justified by her children" (Matthew 11:19b). This may be translated, "wisdom is declared righteous by her works." In other words, you would be wise to look at what I do before judging me an undesirable. In response to one of their questions, "Teacher, which is the great commandant in the law?" (Matthew 22:36), He gave a summary of the entire scriptures:

> Jesus said to him, "You shall love the
> LORD your God with all your heart, with all

your soul, and with all your mind. This is
the first and great commandment. And the
second is like it: 'You shall love your neighbor as yourself.' On these two commandments hang all the Law and the Prophets"
(Matthew 22:37-40).

His great wisdom so confounded them that,

And no one was able to answer Him a word,
nor from that day on did anyone dare question Him anymore (Matthew 22:46).

Jesus' leadership traits, namely: compassion, humility,
impartiality, integrity, trustworthiness, and wisdom, may be
learned and practiced by leaders and aspiring leaders at all
levels. Great wisdom does appear to be genetically
implanted as a gift from God and may set apart great leaders
from other leaders. However, each of us can learn from our
life's experiences and thereby gain some measure of
wisdom. The other leadership traits may come naturally to
some people but I believe that anyone with a willingness to
learn may develop these traits. Feelings will follow attitude
so practicing humility or impartiality, for example, will help
to remove pridefulness and prejudice.

Jesus called us to be perfect, knowing that we will never
attain perfection in this life. Yet He set that goal for each of
us. Likewise, the leadership traits He displayed in His life
are goals for each leader knowing that few of us will ever
fully develop these characteristics.

We now turn to a study of the way Jesus interacted with
His followers, His leadership behaviors.

13

The Very Nature of a Servant

*"We do nothing. He does everything. All glory must be
returned to him. God has not called me to be successful.
He has called me to be faithful."*
—Mother Teresa of Calcutta

How did Jesus interact with His followers? What were His
behaviors as a leader? Earlier we saw that traditional
leadership theories identified a set of leader behaviors that
were characterized as either task-focused or follower-focused.
In other words, leaders were classified as focusing on the
needs of their followers (people-centered) or focusing on job
accomplishment (mission-centered). These studies concluded
that leaders who were more people-centered tended to have
more satisfied followers. However, when faced with difficult
and ambiguous tasks, leaders who were mission-centered
exhibited higher performance. Situational leadership theory

stated that leaders should align their style with the abilities of the people and the demands of the task. Quality leadership theory emphasized respect for the abilities of followers and the importance of involving them in decision-making while achieving high performance through continuous improvement. Greenleaf's servant leader is called into a position of shared leadership due to his servant-like traits. Barna's four leader types are either follower-focused (strategic, team-building) or task-focused (directing, operational).

Jesus' leader behaviors are relational and focused on developing His followers into becoming leaders themselves (Greenleaf's "best test" for leaders). His behaviors may be classified as generally follower-focused without ever losing sight of His mission. Unlike task-focused leaders, He would never sacrifice His followers to accomplish His mission. Rather, *He* would be the sacrifice.

Jesus' Leadership Behaviors

Jesus exhibited ten leadership behaviors as He shaped His small band of future leaders during His three-year ministry. These behaviors are: *obedience, commitment, resisting temptation, exercising authority, providing vision, communication, encouragement, recognizing potential, reconciling, and praying.* We will examine each of these behaviors in detail.

> *"God-like leadership follows this pattern: the divesting of one's power ...in order to invest it in others, so that the end result is the returning of that glory and power to the author."*
> —Leighton Ford

Obedience. First and foremost, Jesus was obedient to the mission set before Him by His Father. Each of us has a boss, someone to whom we report, someone who holds us accountable. That boss might be a supervisor, a board of directors, or the electorate. But virtually everyone works for someone. Jesus was accountable to GOD and his obedience and loyalty never wavered. He operated out of a sense of calling, consistent with Greenleaf's definition of a servant leader (Ford 1991). Jesus was obedient even when it didn't seem to make sense, as when He came to His cousin John for the baptism of repentance. He was sinless yet He consented to be baptized for the forgiveness of sins because His Father had told Him to do so.

> Then Jesus came from Galilee to John at the Jordan to be baptized by him. And John tried to prevent Him, saying, "I need to be baptized by You, and are You coming to me?" But Jesus answered and said to him, "Permit it to be so now, for thus it is fitting for us to fulfill all righteousness." Then he allowed Him (Matthew 3:13-15).

As Jesus and His company were going up to Jerusalem for His fateful encounter with the Jewish and Roman authorities, He told them a third time that He was facing certain death. The mother of James and John approached Him and asked that her two sons might sit on the throne with Him when he came into His kingdom. Jesus replied that such an honor was not His to give but could only be granted by His Father (see Matthew 20:20-23).

Jesus was obedient even unto death. He knew full well the agony He would endure to fulfill GOD's plan, yet He was faithful. In the garden outside Jerusalem He prayed:

"Father, if it is Your will, take this cup away
from Me; nevertheless not My will, but
Yours, be done" (Luke 22:42).

When necessary, a servant leader will sacrifice himself
for the benefit of his followers. This may entail a surrender-
ing of pride, recognition, or reflecting credit to his followers
rather than claiming credit for himself. In some extreme
cases, it may mean giving up one's life for another. Few are
willing to go this far. As Paul argues:

For scarcely for a righteous man will one
die; yet perhaps for a good man someone
would even dare to die (Romans 5:7).

In combat, men die for each other. When all "hell"
breaks loose, the lofty principles that seemed so important
at the beginning are quickly forgotten. Men willingly lay
down their lives for their friends not for their country. The
Congressional Medal of Honor is the nation's highest award
for bravery in combat. Most awards are posthumous and
many are awarded to men who willingly sacrificed their
own lives by falling on a hand grenade to save their
comrades. One such case occurred on February 20, 1945 on
the island of Iwo Jima in the Pacific; only this Marine lived
to tell about it.

Jacklyn Lucas was fourteen when he
enlisted, fooling the recruiters into believing
he was of age. Assigned to drive a truck on
Hawaii, he wanted to fight and stowed away
on a transport headed to Iwo Jima. On D-Day
he landed on the beach without a weapon. He
grabbed one lying on the beach and fought his
way inland. On D+1, Jack and three comrades

were crawling through a trench when eight Japanese sprang up in front of them. Jack shot one of them and then his rifle jammed. As he struggled with it a grenade landed at his feet. He yelled a warning to the others and rammed the grenade into the soft ash. Immediately, another rolled in, Jack Lucas, seventeen, fell on both grenades. "Luke, you're gonna die," he remembered thinking. The force of the explosion blew him up into the air and onto his back. Blood poured out of his mouth and he couldn't move. He knew he was dying.

Miraculously Jack didn't die. He endured twenty-one reconstructive operations and became the nation's youngest Medal of Honor winner—the only high school freshman to receive it. When he was asked fifty-three year later, "Mr. Lucas, why did you jump on those grenades?" he did not hesitate with his answer, "To save my buddies" (Bradley 2000, 174-175).

It was March 30, 1981, and Ronald Reagan had been President of the United States for only nine weeks. He gave a speech that afternoon to the Construction Trades Council at the Washington Hilton Hotel, a short distance from the White House. As he left the hotel at 2:27 p.m., a gunman waited with the press on the sidewalk near the President's limousine. Approaching the open door of the vehicle, Reagan turned to reply to a shouted question from the press when two or three *pop, pops*, rang out. At that moment, two of Reagan's Secret Service agents grabbed him and shoved him to the floor of the waiting limousine's back seat. Agent Tim McCarthy had opened the President's car door and was two or three feet from Reagan when the shots rang out.

Instinctively, he raised his arms and faced in the direction of the gunfire, placing himself between the President and the would-be assassin. He took the next shot in the chest and was punched into the air (Noonan 2001).

The shooting happened so fast—six shots were fired in less than two seconds—that there was no time to think. Instinct and training took over. What would cause a man to jump in front of a bullet meant for another, even if it was his job? Peggy Noonan, in her book, *When Character was King* (2001), observes that President Reagan had a special relationship with his Secret Service Detail:

> "He treated them with equality. He preferred talking with them to talking to the politicians who were in the backseat of the limo with him on the way to the rally. He liked to swap jokes with them and he liked to tease them."
> (Noonan 2001, 176)

Ronald Reagan had established such a close a relationship with these men assigned to protect him that they instinctively placed their own bodies between him and danger fully prepared to suffer the consequences of that action.

Jesus demonstrated this same self-sacrificing love for His friends by dying on a Roman cross.

> But God demonstrates His own love toward us, in that while we were still sinners, Christ died for us (Romans 5:8).

Jesus was obedient to His Father even when GOD turned His face away from Him on the cross as the ultimate atonement for sins. From that cruel tree Jesus cried out to GOD with the words of Psalm 22:

"Eli, Eli, lama sabachthani?" that is, "My
God, My God, why have You forsaken Me?"
And Jesus cried out again with a loud voice,
and yielded up His spirit (Matthew 27:46, 50).

Few of us are required to demonstrate that kind of self-
sacrificing obedience. Yet a servant leader must be willing
to be obedient even when it hurts.

Commitment. Closely associated with obedience is
commitment, or what Deming called constancy of purpose
(Deming 1982). The historian Barbara Tuckman has written
that in her study of great captains the one trait that is
common to all is unwavering commitment—that capacity
for sticking with a goal or mission no matter what the obstacles (Tuchman 1985). There is ample evidence throughout
the New Testament that Jesus understood His mission from
an early age. Certainly, by the time He began His public
ministry, He knew what God required of Him. For three
years He had taught His disciples and prepared them to
assume leadership of His ministry. Now the end was near as
Jesus went up to Jerusalem for the Passover Feast. He had
tried to prepare His disciples for His final scene by twice
describing to them exactly what would happen to Him when
they entered the city. Finally, He "set His face like flint" to
the astonishment of His followers:

Now they were on the road, going up to
Jerusalem, and Jesus was going before them;
and they were amazed. And as they followed
they were afraid. Then He took the twelve
aside again and began to tell them the things
that would happen to Him: "Behold, we are
going up to Jerusalem, and the Son of Man
will be betrayed to the chief priests and to
the scribes; and they will condemn Him to

death and deliver Him to the Gentiles; and
they will mock Him, and scourge Him, and
spit on Him, and kill Him. And the third day
He will rise again" (Mark 10:32-34).

Unlike His followers—or you and I—Jesus knew the
details of His fate yet He was undeterred. His Father had
given Him a mission and He would accomplish that mission
regardless of the cost to Him personally. His commitment
was unequivocal.

The company camped just outside the city walls in a
place called Gethsemane. There Jesus struggled with the
most human of emotions, fear. He feared the coming trials
and the physical pain He would endure but, more impor-
tantly, He feared the separation He knew was coming from
His Father when He took on the sins of the world on the
cross. Three times He prayed to the Father in that garden
that His fate might be altered:

"Father, if it is Your will, take this cup away
from Me; nevertheless not My will, but
Yours, be done" (Luke 22:42).

He was in such agony that, "His sweat became like great
drops of blood falling down to the ground" (Luke 22:44).
Receiving no change in orders from the Father, He determined to complete His mission.

Jesus had ample opportunity to save Himself over the
next two days. Yet, He endured six trials before the Jewish
high council and the Roman authorities. At any point in
these proceedings, He could have denied His claims of
Messiahship and perhaps escaped death. Near the end of His
trials, the Roman governor, Pilate, asked Him if He truly
was the King of the Jews,

Jesus answered, "My kingdom is not of this
world. If My kingdom were of this world,
My servants would fight, so that I should not
be delivered to the Jews; but now My kingdom is not from here" (John 18:36).

Jesus' last words from the cross, "It is finished!" (John
19:30), signify the completion of His mission.

He was committed to the end.

Resisting temptation. Jesus was tempted by the same
temptations each of us face daily. These have not changed
since man was first created and placed in the garden:

• Lust of the flesh (physical)
• Lust of the eyes (emotional, psychological)
• Pride of life (spiritual)

Satan appeared to Jesus during His desert retreat time of
preparation and tried to dissuade Him from the mission GOD
had set before Him. He used these same three temptations:

• Lust of the flesh: "If you are the Son of
God, command this stone to become bread"
(Luke 4:3). He was hungry from His 40-day
fast.
• Lust of the eyes: "All this authority I will
give You, and their glory; for this has
been delivered to me, and I give it to
whomever I wish. Therefore, if You will
worship before me, all will be Yours"
(Luke 4:6, 7).
• Pride of life: "If you are the Son of God,
throw Yourself down from here"
(Luke4:9).

Jesus responded to these temptations of the body,

mind, and spirit by quoting scripture. The Word of GOD defeated Satan and he "departed from Him until an opportune time" (Luke 4:13). Obviously Satan was not finished with tempting Jesus.

Since He was fully man and fully God, Jesus experienced the same temptations that every human faces and yet He remained sinless. Jesus and His disciples were sorely tempted to abandon His mission in the garden of Gethsemane the night of His arrest. On that fateful night, He took His three closest friends from among the disciples and went aside to pray:

> Then He said to them, "My soul is exceedingly sorrowful, even to death. Stay here and watch with Me." He went a little farther and fell on His face, and prayed, saying, "O My Father, if it is possible, let this cup pass from Me; nevertheless, not as I will, but as You will." Then He came to the disciples and found them sleeping, and said to Peter, "What? Could you not watch with Me one hour? Watch and pray, lest you enter into temptation. The spirit indeed is willing, but the flesh is weak" (Matthew 26:38-41).

The temptation to save Himself from the agonizing death He faced was almost overwhelming, yet he surrendered to the will of His Father:

> "O My Father, if this cup cannot pass away from Me unless I drink it, Your will be done" (Matthew 26:42).

Satan was again defeated. But his final defeat would be on the cross.

Exercising authority. A servant leader is not afraid to exercise authority and to make decisions. When possible, she will involve her followers in the decision process. But sometimes the leader is called to make tough decisions alone. The defining elements that determine whether to involve others in the decision process are time and expertise. Knowing that people are generally more committed to decisions that they have had a part in, leaders should try to involve their people in researching and evaluating alternatives. Consensus on a preferred course of action will generally speed implementation. However, when time is critical or the people lack the requisite expertise, the leader must make the decision. Often the only thing worse than a bad decision is no decision at all.

Jesus would often confound the Jewish leaders since He did not conform to the usual rabbinical teaching method. Since the time of Moses, Jewish teachers had developed a rich historical tradition of interpretation of the Law and their application to daily life. Consequently, when a teacher was asked for the meaning of a law, he would refer back to the opinion of rabbi so-and-so who referenced rabbi so-and-so and on back often to Moses. Jesus said that He was the *completion* of the Law:

> "Do not think that I came to destroy the Law
> or the Prophets. I did not come to destroy but
> to fulfill" (Matthew 5:17).

He would often interpret the true meaning of the Law with words like, "You have heard that it was said ..." and then explain what God had intended with a particular law. For example, in the 5th chapter of Matthew we read,

> "You have heard that it was said to those of
> old, 'You shall not commit adultery.' But I

say to you that whoever looks at a woman to
lust for her has already committed adultery
with her in his heart" (Matthew 5:27, 28).

He was saying in effect, "I am the authority. I do not
need to reference rabbi so-and-so." Again, this was a claim
that only God Himself could make and His Jewish listeners
were well aware of that fact.

Jesus demonstrated His authority early in His ministry
beginning immediately after He announced to His hometown that He was the long-awaited messiah. Following His
chilly reception in Nazareth, Jesus went down to the seaside
village of Capernaum and began to teach:

And they were astonished at His teaching,
for His word was with authority (Luke 4:32).

Not only did He demonstrate His authority over the
interpretation of the Law, He exercised authority over the
elements in the midst of a storm on the Sea of Galilee:

Now when they had left the multitude, they
took Him along in the boat as He was. And
other little boats were also with Him. And a
great windstorm arose, and the waves beat
into the boat, so that it was already filling. But
He was in the stern, asleep on a pillow. And
they awoke Him and said to Him, "Teacher,
do you not care that we are perishing?" Then
He arose and rebuked the wind, and said to
the sea, "Peace, be still!" And the wind ceased
and there was a great calm. And they feared
exceedingly, and said to one another, "Who
can this be, that even the wind and the sea
obey Him!" (Mark 4:36-39, 41).

He exercised authority over evil spirits and over disease by casting out demons and healing all manner of sicknesses. He even claimed authority over the Sabbath.

> Now it happened that He went through the grain fields on the Sabbath; and as they went His disciples began to pluck the heads of grain. And the Pharisees said to Him, "Look, why do they do what is not lawful on the Sabbath?" But He said to them, "Have you never read what David did when he was in need and hungry, he and those with him: how he went into the house of God in the days of Abiathar the high priest, and ate the showbread, which is not lawful to eat except for the priests, and also gave some to those who were with him?" And He said to them, "The Sabbath was made for man, and not man for the Sabbath. Therefore the Son of Man is also Lord of the Sabbath" (Mark 2:23-28).

Needless to say, the Jewish leaders were astounded at His audacity and demanded to know,

> "By what authority are You doing these things? And who gave you this authority?" (Matthew 21:23b).

Jesus responded with a question for them regarding the authenticity of John's baptism. When they were unable to answer His question, He replied,

> "Neither will I tell you by what authority I do these things" (Matthew 21:27b).

Jesus exercised His authority with compassion. His character reflected an inner balance of simplicity and integrity (Ford 1991).

Providing vision. Jesus was a visionary. He lived in the moment but pointed to the future. Earlier, we examined the need for a leader to develop a set of guiding principles that included a vision for the organization. In chapter 9, we reviewed Jesus' vision for His ministry. He reiterated time and again that vision throughout His three-year ministry until it truly became a shared vision beginning with His call to the first disciples,

> "Follow Me, and I will make you fishers of men" (Matthew 4:19).

He would paint a picture for His followers using words and images and describe the role that they would play in the coming kingdom:

> "And I also say to you that you are Peter, and on this rock I will build My church, and the gates of Hades shall not prevail against it" (Matthew 16:18).

He foresaw Satan's defeat when He had sent out the seventy disciples with instructions to heal the sick and cast out evil spirits. He rejoiced with them as they returned with news that,

> "Lord, even the demons are subject to us in Your name." And He said to them, "I saw Satan fall like lightning from heaven" (Luke 10:17, 18).

Jesus explained to His disciples how the present related

to the past and the past with the future:

> "Blessed are the eyes which see the things
> you see; for I tell you that many prophets and
> kings have desired to see what you see, and
> have not seen it, and to hear what you hear,
> and have not heard it" (Luke 10:23, 24).

Often the future can be frightening. Fear of the unknown strikes every man. Jesus' followers were fearful for many reasons, not the least of which was that He told them He would be killed when they went up to Jerusalem. But, He assured them that they should not fear the future because He would always care for them. He painted a vision of shelter and refreshment:

> "Let not your heart be troubled; you believe
> in God, believe also in Me. In My Father's
> house are many mansions; if it were not so, I
> would have told you. I go to prepare a place
> for you. And if I go and prepare a place for
> you, I will come again and receive you to
> Myself; that where I am, there you may be
> also" (John 14:1-3).

Jesus described in great detail the events and signs that would precede His Second Coming (see Matthew 24:4-35 and Luke 21:8-36) and although no one knew the exact time for these events (see Matthew 24:36), His arrival would be witnessed by everyone:

> "Then the sign of the Son of Man will appear
> in heaven, and then all the tribes of the earth
> will mourn, and they will see the Son of Man
> coming on the clouds of heaven with power

and great glory" (Matthew 24:30).

A vision becomes empowering when followers share it; when they too can see the vision and are led by it. Luke records how Jesus' vision was reinforced to the disciples by two strangers following His ascension:

> And while they looked steadfastly toward heaven as He went up, behold, two men stood by them in white apparel, who also said, "Men of Galilee, why do you stand gazing up into heaven? This same Jesus, who was taken up from you into heaven, will so come in like manner as you saw Him go into heaven" (Acts 1:10, 11).

Proof that His followers shared Jesus' vision is readily apparent in the writings of the authors of the epistles but foremost in the dedication to that vision even unto death—beginning with His first disciples—by countless believers down through the ages.

14

Let Your Light So Shine

*"Do nothing out of selfish ambition or vain conceit, but in
humility consider others better than yourselves. Each of
you should look not only to your own interests,
but also to the interests of others."*
—Philippians 2:3, 4

In the last chapter, we examined Jesus' first five behaviors
of obedience, commitment, resisting temptation, exercising
authority, and providing vision. In this chapter, we will review
the remaining five behaviors: *communication, encouragement, recognizing potential, reconciling, and praying.*

Communicator. Most leadership studies have
concluded that being a good communicator is a necessary
behavior for successful leadership. The best leaders will
communicate to their followers using a variety of methods
and means. Some leaders are limited in their communication methods by the mission or the size of the organization.
For very large and dispersed organizations, personal one-

on-one communications, albeit effective, is impractical. Therefore, modern communications techniques including electronic mail, instant messaging, video-conferencing, videotape and the Internet (websites, electronic bulletin boards, chat rooms, etc.) are becoming widely used by leaders. Regardless of the means, the enduring principles of persuasion, as taught by Aristotle, remain today: *logos, ethos*, and *pathos*.

- *Logos* is the essence of the message itself. What is the main point or points that should be conveyed? Are they clearly stated? Is the message important?
- *Ethos* is the credibility of the messenger. Who is delivering the message and why? What expertise does this messenger have regarding the message? Is it believable?
- *Pathos* relates to the hearers. Does the message appeal to the inner motives of the listeners? Why should they consider the message important? What impact does it have upon them?

Good communicators pay attention to these principles regardless of the means or methods of communication.

> *"In Jesus' style there are no exaggerations or mannerisms which lend themselves to parody. Jesus can be denied and insulted and blasphemed, but he is still strangely immune to ridicule. After 2000 years his words retain the power to convert.*
> *—Joseph Sobran*

Leighton Ford (1991) suggests nine communication imperatives based on Aristotle's principles:

1. *Clarity of speech comes from clarity of purpose*: know where you are headed (logos). One of Stephen Covey's Seven Habits (1989) is to begin with the end in mind. This means you must understand your vision or goal and work backwards. Ask the question: Now that I know what I hope to achieve or where I want to go, what will it take to get there? As the cat in Wonderland said to Alice, "If you don't know where you're going, it doesn't matter which road you take."

2. *Believability comes in direct proportion to a quiet sense of confidence*: know your source and your identity (ethos). Leaders as communicators must know their business and know themselves. Mastery of self is foremost before a person can hope to lead others. Covey calls this working from the inside out.

3. *Words live forever; therefore, they must be handled with care*: know the power of language (pathos). Perhaps the greatest communicator of the past century was Winston Churchill. He clearly understood the power of language and would spend hours agonizing over each word in his speeches to the Parliament and the British nation. His words still live today and are just as inspiring as when they were spoken half a century ago. Conversely, James, the brother of Jesus, warns us of the power of an unbridled tongue:

   > Even so the tongue is a little member and boasts great things. See how great a forest

> a little fire kindles! But no
> man can tame the tongue. It is
> an unruly evil, full of deadly
> poison (James 3:5, 8).

4. *How they hear is as important as what you say*: know your audience (pathos). A good communicator will speak at a level and with terms and illustrations that are understandable to his audience.

5. *Having the truth is only half the battle*: know your craft (logos). Careful selection of means and methods will help to ensure that the message is received. Good communicators will take advantage of a variety of methods to retain interest and insure that the message is received.

6. *Knowing when is as important as knowing what to say*: know your timing (logos). As they say in show business, "Timing is everything!" Good communication involves both sending and receiving. A message is not communicated unless it is received by the intended audience with the intended meaning. Knowing when to speak and what to say when is critically important in sending messages that will be received.

7. *Simplicity means to say one thing well*: know your point (logos). Lee Iacocca once said, "The main thing is to keep the main thing the main thing." Or, as one automobile manufacturer boasts: "Do one thing. Do it well." Good communicators understand that it is better to focus on a small number of points and to drive them home then to address many points that won't be remembered.

8. *Take your calling seriously, but do not be anxious for yourself*: know where your responsibility begins and ends (ethos). Paul reminds us to,

> Be anxious for nothing, but in everything by prayer and supplication, with thanksgiving, let your requests be made known to God; and the peace of God, which surpasses all understanding, will guard your hearts and minds through Christ Jesus (Philippians 4:6, 7).

A Christian communicator understands that his job is to communicate the message in the best way he knows how and then to leave the results to God.

9. *Never underestimate your opposition but always count on your hidden resource*: know your enemy and know your ally (ethos). We know that our "… adversary the devil walks about like a roaring lion, seeking whom he may devour" (1 Peter 5:8). Therefore, we must be vigilant and anticipate that our message will be distorted and misunderstood. The Good News is that we have One who promised to never leave us nor forsake us. Depend upon Him.

Jesus was a master communicator. He clearly understood the principles of persuasion and good communication. From his study of Jesus' communication technique, Bruce Wilkerson (1994) argues that Jesus used seven teaching methods: lecture, stories and illustrations, visual aids, questions and answers, discussion, drama, and projects.

- Lecture, surprisingly, was the most widely used communication technique. When God spoke to His people it was usually with a lecture. As a college educator, I tried to avoid the traditional lecture method as much as possible. Yet I found that although I tried to add stories and illustrations, questions and answers, drama, and projects to my presentations, still much of the classroom time is spent lecturing. This was not a bad thing it just should not be the only method for communicating.

- Jesus used stories and illustrations 65% of the time. Most of these were parables using the everyday experiences of the people to illustrate a teaching point. Many of these related to describing the indescribable: "The kingdom of heaven is like ..." and then He would use a common event, like sowing seed, putting yeast in flour, or hiding a great treasure. Good teachers know this technique and will illustrate their main point with a story. Long after the teaching point is forgotten, listeners will recall a well-chosen story. Jesus used various sources for His stories including personal experience, history, the Scriptures, and His imagination. Again, surprisingly, most of His stories came from His imagination. And that was why they were so compelling: you never knew where He was going!

- Visual aids are an important communication method. Communicators who do not understand the power of visual graphics are overlooking a critical and necessary method for communication. Young people today have grown up with video and computer technologies with ever-more complex visual graphics. Some have argued that the attention span of pre-teens in our society is no more than 15 minutes without some form of visual stimulation. I have found in my own teaching that unless I use a variety of visual aids to supplement my lectures, my students lose interest. Jesus understood this teaching method and would use visual aids available to Him, like a seed or a fish, to illustrate His teaching. God taught the Israelites the importance of visual aids as recorded in the book of Deuteronomy:

> Now this is the commandment, and these are the statutes and judgments which the LORD your God has commanded to teach you, that you may observe them in the land which you are crossing over to possess ... You shall bind them as a sign on your hand, and they shall be as frontlets between your eyes (Deuteronomy 6:1, 8).

- Jesus used questions and answers, or the dialectic method of teaching. Typically, when He was asked a question, He would reply with a question of His own. People, especially adults, seem to learn best when the answer comes out of their own mouths. This technique has been used since at least the time of Aristotle and Plato and is just as effective today. Jesus understood that learning occurs through guiding students with a set of carefully constructed questions toward discovery of the central truth.

- Discussion often follows questions and is also an important communication method. Students will often learn from each other better than even the most gifted teacher alone can provide. The key to effective discussion as a teaching method is having a set of ground rules that encourage questions and opinions, no matter how crazy they may sound, without criticism from anyone else.

- Jesus used drama to illustrate His most important teaching points. As He stood in front of His friend Lazarus' tomb, He prayed,

> "Father, I thank You that You have heard Me. And I know that You always hear Me, but because of the people who are standing by I said this, that they may believe that You sent Me" (John 11:41b, 42).

The dramatic appearance of a man bound in burial clothes beckoned by the words: "Lazarus, come forth!" (John 11:43) would not be quickly forgotten. Likewise, when Jesus had tried many times to communicate to His disciples that they were to be a different kind of leader, one who would be servant first, and they just could not seem to understand, He employed drama to make an unforgettable point:

> Jesus ... rose from supper and laid aside His garments, took a towel and girded Himself. After that, He poured water into a basin and began to wash

the disciples' feet, and to wipe them
with the towel with which He was
girded (John 13:4, 5).

- Projects are an effective teaching method *provided*
  you have the end in mind before you begin. An
  open-ended project will often disappoint both
  student and teacher. Jesus used well-supervised
  projects to teach His disciples such as when He sent
  out the twelve disciples and later seventy others to
  minister to the people Luke 9:1, 10:1).

Encouragement. The best leaders are encouragers. This
is true in the family as well as in our professional lives. It is
a self-fulfilling prophecy that a child who grows up with
affirmation will have a positive self-image. Conversely, a
child that is raised with constantly negative characteriza-
tions will develop low self-esteem and often becomes a
scourge to society.

My office at Montreat backed on the gymnasium. The
women's basketball coach was a great encourager and I
always knew when his team was practicing by the continual
stream of encouragement that penetrated my office walls:
"Great shot, Crystal." "Nice block, Sis." "Way to hustle,
ladies!" His teams were successful, in part, because he was
able to get his players to go beyond what they thought they
were capable of through his encouragement.

Jesus was a great encourager as He prepared His followers to go beyond what they thought they were capable of and
to reach for the future He promised them. He characterized
them as the people that preserve and brighten the world:

"You are the salt of the earth ... You are the
light of the world ... Let your light so shine
before men, that they may see your good

works and glorify your Father in heaven"
(Matthew 5:13, 14, 16).

When they were fearful, He encouraged them:

"Take courage! It is I; do not be afraid"
(Matthew 14:27).

When his followers began to feel sorry for themselves,
He reassured them with the promise of a better life to come:

"Assuredly I say to you, that in the regenera-
tion, when the Son of Man sits on the throne
of His glory, you who have followed Me will
also sit on twelve thrones, judging the twelve
tribes of Israel. And everyone who has left
houses or brothers or sisters or father or
mother or wife or children or lands, for My
name's sake, shall receive a hundredfold,
and inherit eternal life" (Matthew 19:28, 29).

Again, He encouraged them regarding faith, one time
using a withered fig tree as a visual aid:

"Assuredly, I say to you, if you have faith
and do not doubt, you will not only do what
was done to the fig tree, but also if you say to
this mountain, 'Be removed and be cast into
the sea,' it will be done. And whatever things
you ask in prayer, believing, you will
receive" (Matthew 21:21, 22).

That last evening that Jesus spent with His disciples was
full of encouragement. He promised those that had left all
they had for Him that although they would be persecuted in

the days and years ahead, He would "... not leave you orphans; I will come to you" (John 14:18). He said He would send them

> "... the Helper, the Holy Spirit, whom the Father will send in My name, He will teach you all things, and bring to your remembrance all things that I said to you" (John 14:26).

He explained that although He was going away, "... but I will see you again" (John 16:22), and then He prayed that the Father would strengthen them and protect them from the temptations of the world:

> "I pray for them. I do not pray for the world but for those whom You have given Me, for they are Yours. I do not pray that You should take them out of the world, but that You should keep them from the evil one" (John 17:9, 15).

Finally, after the resurrection, when Jesus appeared to the disciples to give them the charge known as the Great Commission, He left them with these words of encouragement:

> "Lo, I am with you always, even to the end of the age" (Matthew 28:20).

Recognize potential. In chapter 10 we discussed Jesus' five-phase strategy including picking potential leaders. He truly looked beyond the outward appearance of people and looked deep into their hearts. He recognized a potential leader when others saw only an uneducated fisherman, a traitorous tax collector, or a hotheaded zealot. He saw the potential in people, trained them, encouraged them, and empowered them to become the leaders He knew they would become.

He called Simon and his brother Andrew as they cast their nets into the sea and said,

> "Follow Me, and I will make you fishers of
> men" (Matthew 4:19).

Two other fishermen, James and John, were called likewise (Matthew 4:21). He saw a Jew named Levi sitting at the tax office and said, "Follow Me", and he did (Mark 2:14). He even went so far as to accept a dinner invitation at this man's house where other notorious sinners gathered. When the scribes and Pharisees caught wind of this, they began to grumble among themselves,

> "How is it that He eats and drinks with tax
> collectors and sinners?" When Jesus heard it,
> He said to them, "Those who are well have
> no need of a physician, but those who are
> sick. I did not come to call the righteous, but
> sinners to repentance" (Mark 2:16, 17).

Simon is probably my favorite disciple. Impetuous Peter, the one who wanted to walk on water. The one who, in his confusion, wanted to *do* something on the Mount of Transfiguration when he saw Moses and Elijah with Jesus, so he offered to build shelters for them. The one who tried to dissuade Jesus from going up to Jerusalem. The one who said he would die before he would forsake Jesus. The one who lashed out with his sword. The one who denied he even knew Him. The one who put *on* his clothes and dove into the sea when he recognized the risen Jesus on the shore. The one whom Jesus asked three times, "Simon, son of Jonah, do you love me?" This same weak man would answer Jesus' question, "But who do you say that I am?" by declaring, "You are the Christ, the Son of the living God" (Matthew 16:15, 16). And on this response, Jesus said, He would build His church:

> "Blessed are you, Simon Bar-Jonah, for flesh and blood has not revealed this to you, but My Father who is in heaven. And I also say to you that you are Peter, and on this rock I will build My church, and the gates of Hades shall not prevail against it" (Matthew 16:17, 18).

Jesus knew that Peter would betray Him and yet He also knew that he would eventually become a leader in His church.

> And the Lord said, "Simon, Simon! Indeed, Satan has asked for you, that he may sift you as wheat. But I have prayed for you, that your faith should not fail; and when you have returned to Me, strengthen your brethren" (Luke 22:31, 32).

Peter, of course, did become one of the principle leaders in the new Christian church and died a martyr's death at the hands of the Roman emperor Nero. According to early church tradition when informed of his impending crucifixion, Peter asked to be crucified upside down saying he was unworthy to die in the same manner as his Lord.

Reconciling. Dealing with conflict is an inevitable and important function of leadership. Conflict correctly and positively adjudicated can produce strength and unity; while conflict improperly resolved or ignored can fester and rot an organization from the core outward. Viktor Frankl, an Austrian psychiatrist and holocaust survivor, wrote about the ways in which Jewish inmates of Hitler's concentration camps met their suffering. He wrote that people could bring meaning to some of the most inhumane circumstances by the ways in which they chose to react to them (Ford 1991).

Jesus recognized three types of conflict: *unavoidable, essential*, and *incidental*. When faced with unavoidable conflict, He would seize the opportunity to confront and then withdraw. He considered essential conflict an opportunity to teach and develop people. He would first identify the root cause of the conflict and then move the conflict to common ground. He would leave the conflicted parties with a common understanding of the nature of the conflict and how to overcome it. However, when faced with incidental conflict, He would often bypass or postpone dealing with it recognizing that the time required to resolve the conflict detracted from the important tasks at hand (Ford 1991).

Jesus taught that when there is conflict we are to seek reconciliation. He does not place the responsibility only upon the one who has done the offending:

> "Therefore if you bring your gift to the altar, and there remember that your brother has something *against you*, leave your gift there before the altar, and go your way. First be reconciled to your brother, and then come and offer your gift. Agree with your adversary quickly, while you are on the way with him, lest your adversary deliver you to the judge, the judge hand you over to the officer, and you be thrown into prison" (Matthew 5:23-25 *emphasis added*).

His picture of reconciliation is completely out of focus

with the world's image. He taught not to seek revenge and not to hate your enemies. Rather, He called His disciples to be more like God the Father who loves the just and the unjust.

> "You have heard that it was said, 'An eye for an eye and a tooth for a tooth.' But I tell you not to resist an evil person. But whoever slaps you on your right cheek, turn the other to him also. If anyone wants to sue you and take away your tunic, let him have your cloak also. And whoever compels you to go one mile, go with him two. Give to him who asks you, and from him who wants to borrow from you do not turn away.
>
> "You have heard that it was said, 'You shall love your neighbor and hate your enemy.' But I say to you, love your enemies, bless those who curse you, do good to those who hate you, and pray for those who spitefully use you and persecute you, that you may be sons of your Father in heaven" (Matthew 6:38-45).

These radical words must have stunned his disciples, just as they remain shocking today. Jesus calls us to reconciliation with those who would do us harm as well as those who are our friends and family. He calls us into relationship with each other and reminds us that all relationships must first build upon Him.

> "Do not think that I came to bring peace on earth. I did not come to bring peace but a sword. For I have come to set a man against his father, a daughter against her mother, and a daughter-in-law against her mother-in-law;

and 'a man's enemies will be those of his own household.' He who loves father or mother more than Me is not worthy of Me. And he who loves son or daughter more than Me is not worthy of Me. And he who does not take his cross and follow after Me is not worthy of Me. He who finds his life will lose it, and he who loses his life for My sake will find it" (Matthew 10:34-39).

These too are radical words that shake us to the core. Jesus wants first place in our lives and all other relationships, personal and professional, must build outward from that relationship. This is illustrated in the set of concentric circles below (Figure 14-1).

Figure 14-1 Our Relationships

> *"Your attitude should be the same as that of Christ Jesus: Who, being in very nature God, did not consider equality with God something to be grasped, but made himself nothing, taking the very nature of a servant, being made in human likeness."*
> —*Philippians 2:5-11*

Prays. Above all other behaviors, Jesus prayed. He said that He did nothing on His own accord but only what He saw the Father doing. He maintained a running dialogue with His Father. We have recorded in the New Testament mainly His "big decision" prayers but we can be assured that He was constantly in communication with God, His Abba, as we see in His prayer before the tomb of Lazarus:

"Father, I thank You that You have heard Me. *And I know that You always hear Me*, but because of the people who are standing by I said this, that they may believe that You sent Me" (John 11:41b, 42 *emphasis added*).

Before He chose His disciples,

He went out to the mountain to pray, and continued all night in prayer to God (Luke 5:12).

Many times Jesus would seek the Father's face to "recharge his batteries" after a time of particularly demanding teaching or healing. Often He would go up "to the mountain to pray" (Mark 6:46, Matthew 14:23) or try to retire to a secluded place away from the crushing crowds

(Matthew 14:13). Frequently, His rest was soon disturbed when the crowds discovered where He had gone. "Moved with compassion," He would minister to their needs (Matthew 14:14).

His disciples were often the subjects of Jesus' prayers. When the seventy disciples returned joyfully from their first "project," Jesus rejoiced in the Spirit,

> "I thank You, Father, Lord of heaven and earth, that You have hidden these things from the wise and prudent and revealed them to babes. Even so, Father, for so it seemed good in Your sight (Luke 10:21).

During the Last Supper, Jesus prayed for Himself, for His disciples, and for all those who would believe in His name in the centuries to come:

> "I do not pray that You should take them out of the world, but that You should keep them from the evil one. I do not pray for these alone, but also for those who will believe in Me through their word" (John 17:15, 20).

On that fateful night when He was betrayed, Jesus went out of the city with His disciples to the Mount of Olives to a place called Gethsemane. Knowing what lay before Him, being fully human and yet fully divine, He prayed that the Father would not require of Him what He knew must come:

> "O My Father, if it is possible, let this cup pass from Me; nevertheless, not as I will, but as You will" (Matthew 26:39).

Luke, the beloved physician, records that His agony was such that,

> His sweat became like great drops of blood falling down to the ground (Luke 22:44).

Obedient until the end, Jesus accepted the fate prescribed before hand for Him and roused His sleeping disciples as his betrayers approached:

> "Rise, let us be going. See, My betrayer is at hand" (Matthew 26:46).

Jesus was in constant communication with the Father through prayer. He heard and obeyed the voice of God even when, in His flesh, He recoiled against what God was asking of Him.

Sometimes the still, small voice of God will speak to you when you least expect it.

The Department of Defense had a long-standing policy of funding morale, welfare, and recreation (MWR) functions on its installations with an operating budget augmented from Washington. In my first year in command of a Marine Corps air station, we were notified that in the upcoming fiscal year this funding would cease and that all MWR activities would have to become self-sufficient or close. I met with the head of the MWR department and charged him with development of a plan to reduce overall expenses while maintaining a high level of service in light of the coming budgetary realignment.

MWR operated a number of revenue-generating activities (retail stores, service stations, clubs, bowling alley, transient facility) that would have to produce enough income to fund the non-revenue-generating recreation activities (gym, weight room, pools, etc.). Over the next several months, I reviewed the plans and monthly reports that indicated that all was going well.

One morning, the head of our internal auditing branch walked into my office and declared, "Colonel, I don't think you know what's going on around here!" Surprised and not a little defensive, I said, "What do you mean, I don't know what's going on?"

He proceeded to tell me that over coffee that morning the assistant MWR officer had told him that for the last several months MWR had been cashing in CDs early and with a penalty, to meet their payroll. He said that they had just cashed their last CD. He estimated that they were losing about $50,000 a month.

"How much time do we have left," I asked.

"No more than 60 days but it may be as few as 30 days," he replied.

When the auditor left my office, I immediately called for the MWR officer. Naturally, he was out of town on a business trip. It took two more days before he returned and by that time I was really burning!

When the MWR officer walked through the door of my office, I raised up out of my seat, pointed my finger at him and shouted, "You're fired!" His reaction was not what I expected.

"Please don't do this to me, Colonel. This is my last chance. I've been passed over for promotion, my wife is leaving me; I have no self-respect left. If you fire me now, I have nothing left to live for. Please give me another chance," he pleaded.

I really wanted to reach across my desk and choke him but a little voice whispered in my ear and said, "Tell him the Good News." No, I argued, not him! Look what he's done to this installation. We will probably have to lay people off and the Marines and their families will lose a lot of recreation services. "Tell him!" the voice said.

So I did.

"Phil, there is only one thing you can do at this point to redeem your life," I said.

"What's that?" he asked.

"You need to surrender your life to Jesus Christ and make Him your Lord and Master. He will save your life. Do you want to do that, now?" I asked.

Just five minutes earlier, I wanted to humiliate this man who had blatantly violated the trust I had placed in him. But that little voice whispered in my ear that I was just like him, no better, no worse. "Tell him the Good News, He said." A minute later, we were kneeling together around the coffee table in my office as he prayed the sinner's prayer.

I did relieve Phil of his duties but I did it in such a way that he could maintain his dignity. He joined a Bible study group that met in our home until his retirement. He is now happily remarried and flying for a major airline. I hear from him each year at Christmas. His message often contains these words, "Thank you so much. You are always in my prayers."

A leader who is open to the Father may hear the voice of God at the most unexpected times. Following the example of Jesus, our response should be, "Nevertheless not my will but Yours be done."

> *"Your attitude should be the same as that of Christ Jesus: Who, being in very nature God, did not consider equality with God something to be grasped, but made himself nothing, taking the very nature of a servant, being made in human likeness."*
> *—Philippians 2:5-11*

Jesus' Leadership Summarized

How would you describe Jesus Christ as a servant leader? He was a man of great compassion and humility born of adversity. His character was such that all knew Him as a man of integrity who was trustworthy, a man of His word. Although He was not formally educated, He demonstrated great knowledge and wisdom from an early age. As a leader, He was obedient and loyal to His Superior, even when that obedience meant He would forfeit His life. He overcame temptation throughout His life and remained focused on His mission. He was committed to that vision and mission which His Father had showed Him and would not be turned aside regardless of the consequences. He was a great communicator who understood his audiences and used a variety of methods to communicate His message.

Recognizing the potential within a small group of future leaders, He enabled them and then empowered them to assume the mantle of leadership. He did not hesitate to exercise authority while continually reminding them of His vision for the future. He was a superb motivator who encouraged His future leaders through trial and error and personal leadership. He understood the value of conflict and would deliberately choose to use conflict to illustrate an important teaching point. He was a reconciler who brought people from different backgrounds, beliefs, and values to a common understanding. Overall, He maintained constant communication with the Father who guided Him throughout His life. He came to serve and not to be served. Jesus was a servant first.

Now that we have examined Jesus' strategy, His leadership traits and behaviors, we turn to His tactics. How did He implement His strategies?

15

Blessed are the Peacemakers

And the Lord's servant must not quarrel; instead, he must be kind to everyone, able to teach, not resentful. Those who oppose him he must gently instruct, in the hope that God will grant them repentance leading them to a of the truth, and that they will come to their senses and escape from the trap of the devil, who has taken them captive to do his will.
—2 Timothy 2:24-26

Jesus' Tactics

In chapter 10 we examined Jesus five-phased strategy: preparation; picking potential leaders; enabling them; empowering them; and finally, deploying them. What tactics did He use to implement His strategy? As we answer that question we will discover that these same tactics are available to leaders today.

Jesus' implementation was eloquently simple and straightforward. His five major tactics were:
1. *Teaching*
2. *Leading by example*
3. *Delegating*
4. *Removing fear*
5. *Forgiving mistakes*

Teaching. Leadership at all levels requires teaching. The more senior one becomes in an organization, the more teaching one does. As we discovered in the last chapter, Jesus was a master teacher who used a variety of methods and means to get His message across. He used three *levels* of teaching:
1. Direct one-on-one
2. Small group
3. Public teaching

Direct one-on-one teaching occurs within the leadership group. It may be focused on a few marked for future senior leadership but others within the leadership group will also be beneficiaries of personal instruction. This may take the form of mentoring or discipleship: i.e., a deliberate, planned effort at development of specific leadership skills. It is much more than a once-a-year performance review.

In the Gospels, Jesus is recorded as giving Peter, John, James and Thomas personal one-on-one instruction. We know from history that these men became the senior leaders within the nascent Christian church. No doubt, others within the small group of twelve disciples also received this type of tailored instruction from time to-time.

In order to provide direct one-on-one teaching a leader must invest *time* in his followers. Jesus' future leaders lived with Him. They saw Him when He was up; and they saw Him when He was discouraged. They saw Him when He awoke with matted hair and morning breath. They saw Him in the evening when He was tired and spent from the day. And He saw them. He saw their quarreling and jealousy. He saw their pettiness and pridefulness. But He also saw their potential. And He taught each one how to be a leader with instruction tailored to the needs of that person.

Small group teaching focuses primarily on leadership team development. It is directed at preparing a group of future leaders by giving them "insider information" that the general public does not have and establishing trust and confidence within the group and with the leader. Through small group teaching, the leader establishes a critical mass of future leaders who are committed to the vision, mission and values of the organization. These are the people whom will assume the mantel of leadership when the leader departs.

Jesus' private teaching to his small group of future leaders was pointedly aimed at preparing them for the trials they would face in the not-to-distant future. Three times He taught,

> them that the Son of Man must suffer many things, and be rejected by the elders and chief priests and scribes, and be killed, and after three days rise again. He spoke this word openly (Mark 8:31, 32).

He warned them of the events to come and that He would be killed; but He also assured them that He would be resurrected to life. This was a fundamental truth that was central to His ministry. These future leaders needed to understand that truth and believe it in order to persevere through the troubled times which lay ahead of them. He needed their total commitment not simply their compliance.

Some of His teaching was hard to comprehend and as a result many left Him. When He was asked what sign would

He give the people so that they might believe in Him, like the *manna* God provided in the wilderness, He likened Himself to

> "the living bread which came down from heaven. If anyone eats of this bread, he will live forever; and the bread that I shall give is My flesh, which I shall give for the life of the world. Most assuredly, I say to you, unless you eat the flesh of the Son of Man and drink His blood, you have no life in you" (John 6:51, 53).

> Therefore many of His disciples, when they heard this, said, "This is a hard saying; who can understand it?" From that time many of His disciples went back and walked with Him no more (John 6:60, 66).

When teaching in public, He would speak in parables. But when He taught His disciples in private, He spoke plainly:

> "To you it has been given to know the mysteries of the kingdom of God, but to the rest it is given in parables" (Luke 8:10).

> "And when they were alone, He explained all things to His disciples" (Mark 4:34).

Public teaching is directed at followers. These are people who have been attracted to hear the leader for a variety of reasons but they have no real commitment. They are often seeking a "sign," some performance, action, or visible proof that what the leader says has validity. Members of an organization may be enrolled, i.e., complying with the rules and regulations of the organization, yet they lack commitment to the norms and long-range objectives of the organization.

Consistent with the custom of the day, when Jesus went to a new town He would teach in the local synagogue. When the crowds became too large, he moved outside and used a natural setting for His pulpit such as a mountainside or from a fishing boat facing the shore. He would vary His teaching style depending on His audience.

About one third of Jesus' teaching was in parables, which are brief stories from everyday life told by way of analogy to illustrate spiritual truths. Jesus' chose the things around Him and known to His listeners to illustrate His parables; e.g., sowing seed, weeds in the garden, yeast in dough, a hidden treasure, a fisherman's net. Because Biblical truths were illustrated by way of these stories, the people would easily remember them and could repeat them to their family and friends.

His teaching was radical because the values He taught were markedly different from the norms of His culture. Therefore, He would often repeat a lesson using a different illustration; e.g., "the kingdom of heaven is like ..." (see Matthew 13:24-33). Perhaps His best know teaching was delivered in a natural mountainside amphitheater and known as The Sermon on the Mount (see Matthew 5:1-7:29). Here He taught his followers how they were to live their lives in community with one another and how they were to obey the revealed will of God.

Public teaching is aimed at inculcating the vision, mission, and values of the organization. The language of public teaching must match the audience and frequent illustrations and stories make the teaching memorable.

Leading by example. Jesus said, "I am the way, the truth, and the life." He said this in response to Thomas' question, "Lord, we do not know where You are going, and how can we know the way?" (John 14:5, 6). Obviously, this statement has significance with regard to eternal salvation but it also implies that Jesus is claiming He is the model for His disciples to follow. These words were spoken near the end of Jesus' earthly mission but they were certainly not the first time He had demonstrated to His disciples leadership by example. He had shown His disciples daily over the past three years how to put into practice the values He taught: to love God and to love your neighbor as yourself, to not take offense, to respect those in authority, to live in peace with all men, to consider the needs of others before your own.

Incredibly the disciples still did not get it! After three intensive years of instruction His disciples quarreled at the Last Supper over who would be the greatest in the kingdom of God. Short of time and needing to illustrate the type of leadership He expected in an unforgettable way, Jesus got up from supper and removed His outer garments:

> He poured water into a basin and began to wash the disciples' feet, and to wipe them with the towel with which He was girded (John 13:5).

Over the protestations of Peter, He assumed the duties of the lowliest house servant. When He had finished,

> He said to them, "Do you know what I have done to you? You call Me Teacher and Lord, and you say well, for so I am. If I then, your Lord and Teacher, have washed your feet, you also ought to wash one another's feet. *For I have given you an example*, that you should do as I have done to you" (John 13:12-15, *emphasis added*).

Jesus had one more illustration to play out on a hill called Golgotha. He said that the law and the prophets hang on the commandments of love:

> "'You shall love the LORD your God with all your heart, with all your soul, and with all your mind.' "This is the first and great commandment. And the second is like it: 'You shall love your neighbor as yourself'" (Matthew 22:37, 39).

Jesus went to the cross as an example of love for His followers and in obedience to His Father. He was setting an example for His disciples to emulate. His Father told Him that He must give up His life as atonement for the sins of the world so that man might be reconciled to God. And He obeyed. He could have called down "more than twelve legions of angels" to rescue Him but that would mean putting His will above His Father's will. That He would not do.

> *I asked Jesus, "How much do you love me?" "This much," He answered, and He stretched out His arms and died.*
> —*Anonymous*

Delegating. Jesus understood the need to delegate. He first *enabled* His disciples through His teaching and small trials that were thoroughly debriefed and critiqued. When they were ready, he *empowered* them with responsibility, authority, and accountability:

> "He called His twelve disciples to him and *gave them authority* to drive out evil spirits

and to heal every disease and sickness"
(Matthew 10:1 NIV *emphasis added*).

When "five thousand men, besides women and children" who had come out in the wilderness to hear Him teach
were hungry, rather than call down *manna* from heaven
Himself, He said to His disciples, "You give them something to eat" (Matthew 14:16). He resisted the temptation to
take the easy way out and just do the job Himself. But He
knew that His disciples would never grow unless they were
given the responsibility for accomplishing the mission. He
had already given them authority to call upon spiritual
resources. And He would hold them accountable by noting
the surplus remaining after everyone had been fed.

Apparently the disciples needed more training for it was
not long before this scene was repeated with "four thousand
men, besides women and children." Following this supper
with only seven loaves of bread and a few little fish, Jesus
asked them again for an accounting:

> "Do you not yet understand, or remember the
> five loaves of the five thousand and how
> many baskets you took up? Nor the seven
> loaves of the four thousand and how many
> large baskets you took up? How is it you do
> not understand that I did not speak to you
> concerning bread?—but to beware of the
> leaven of the Pharisees and Sadducees"
> (Matthew 16:9-11).

Jesus used the feeding of two large groups of hungry
people as a training ground for His disciples to exercise the
authority He had delegated to them. The people's dinner
was their responsibility and He had them account for the
resources used and remaining. He also reminded them that

they would face formidable opposition while exercising the authority He had granted to them.

Jesus used the Parable of the Talents to illustrate the concept of delegation and fulfilling ones responsibility. In this well-known story, three servants are entrusted with their master's wealth "each according to his own ability" while the master was away (Matthew 25:15). Upon the master's return, each servant was held accountable for his investment decisions. Two of the three servants doubled their investment but the third merely returned what had been entrusted to him without any gain. The master praised the two but castigated the third:

> "So you ought to have deposited my money
> with the bankers, and at my coming I would
> have received back my own with interest"
> (Matthew 25:27).

This story clearly illustrates the three elements of delegation:

1. *Responsibility*: each was given a sum to invest in accordance with their ability.
2. *Authority*: each could invest as they saw fit.
3. *Accountability*: each was held accountable for the results of their investment decisions.

A common mistake made by many leaders is failing to hold subordinates accountable. As this next story will illustrate, where there is no accountability, productivity improvements and efficiency will often slip away.

> Faced with having to compete against
> private contractors for jobs currently per-
> formed by government employees, I knew
> that we would have to improve productivity

aboard the Air Station if we hoped to offer a competitive bid and have a chance at retaining the facility maintenance functions in-house. We measured productivity by comparing the time it took to perform a certain task, for example: maintenance on a building's HVAC system, against a norm known as Engineering Performance Standards (EPS). Standards were established for all maintenance functions similar to the standards applied to automobile maintenance.

When you ask for an estimate to replace a broken starter motor on your car, the service representative will consult a standards manual that will tell him how many hours it should take to change the starter. He will multiply that hourly figure times his labor rate to determine the labor cost for changing the starter. This is the amount you will pay regardless of how much time it actually takes a mechanic to replace the motor.

Our productivity was running at about 1.5 to 2.0 times EPS. In other words, we were using up to twice the standard amount of time to perform maintenance functions. I knew that this would not be competitive against a private contractor. Our challenge was to drive our productivity below the EPS standard.

After several months of experimentation, reengineering, and process improvement, we were able to double our productivity to about 0.8 EPS or 20% less than the standard. This made us very competitive and we won the head-to-head competition with a large private firm and retained the facility maintenance functions in-house.

Managers had delegated responsibility and authority to maintenance personnel who made the process improvements that resulted in greater efficiency and productivity. Our mistake was in not establishing a system to continually measure our productivity. When it was next evaluated, albeit a year later, we had slipped to over 1.0 EPS.

The reductions in cycle time and gains in productivity had been hard to achieve. It was much easier to slide back into the old way of doing things—and that is exactly what happened. Delegation of responsibility and authority without accountability are doomed to failure.

Removing fear. W. Edwards Deming understood the principle taught by Jesus that for people to experience joy in their work you must drive out fear and remove barriers that rob people of pride in workmanship. Fear paralyzes people: fear of failing; fear of not knowing the answer; fear of making a mistake; fear of making the wrong decision. Fear is not exclusive to hourly employees. Managers share the same fears as everyone else and it is up to the leader to create a culture where people are not fearful. Fearful people are not creative, innovative, solution-finders. They are stagnant, status quo, backside-covering people.

Jesus recognized the paralyzing power of fear and He is often recorded as saying, "Fear not" to His followers. After a long night of ministry, He was tired and lay down in the stern of a fishing boat as his disciples sailed across the Sea of Galilee away from the press of the crowds:

> "And suddenly a great tempest arose on the
> sea, so that the boat was covered with the
> waves. But He was asleep. Then His disci-
> ples came to Him and awoke Him, saying,
> 'Lord, save us! We are perishing!' But He
> said to them, 'Why are you fearful, O you of
> little faith?' Then He arose and rebuked the
> winds and the sea, and there was a great
> calm" (Matthew 8:24-26).

Jesus brought "a great calm" and peace to a fearful situation. He was trustworthy and His disciples, when they
became fearful, immediately turned to Him for help. They
knew that He would "save" them while He used the experience as a lesson in faith.

Fear of the unknown is perhaps man's greatest fear.
When Jesus took His inner circle of Peter, James and John
with Him up on the mountain and was transfigured before
their eyes, they were filled with fear. They did not understand what had happened to their Master, or how Moses and
Elijah, long dead, could be standing talking to Jesus. And
they had no idea where the voice they clearly heard had
come from.

> "But Jesus came and touched them and said,
> 'Arise, and do not be afraid'" (Matthew 17:7).

By His calm demeanor, Jesus radiated confidence and
quickly dispelled their fears.

> To me the most poignant scene in Steven
> Spielberg's classic film, *Schindler's List*,
> takes place in the basement of the Camp
> Commandant's house, now serving as sleep-
> ing quarters for a young Jewish woman. The

young woman has been removed from the camp barracks and assigned to the position of domestic servant. She has found some favor in the Commandant's eyes owing primarily to her physical beauty. Schindler, searching for a bottle of wine, finds her in the basement and begins to question her about her position. Sensing his compassion, she hesitantly begins to reveal her deep feelings of fear. What she fears most is the uncertainty of her life. She does not know why some people are chosen to die while others live. All the usual rules of life have been thrown out. Her master, without provocation, had just shot an old woman walking across the yard that very morning. She could no longer believe that her good behavior would save her. She didn't know *what* would save her. Life and death had become arbitrary; and her greatest fear was not knowing.

Fear will stymie management's efforts to improve productivity. Employees who are fearful of losing their jobs or causing others to lose theirs will not offer cost or time-saving ideas. Leaders must first remove fear by demonstrating that they are trustworthy.

The process and system improvements described earlier in facility maintenance did not come about easily. The first and greatest obstacle was fear.

I knew through the experiences of other military installations that had already gone through the contracting-out process that we would need to reduce our work force by about 30% in order to be competitive. We called our people together and explained the process and that we wanted their ideas on how to improve productivity. "You know better than anyone what needs to be done around here to become more efficient," I said. "Let's hear your good ideas." I did not share in public the target that I had set for force reduction but the employees feared that we would have to let some people go.

We received *no* suggestions and no new ideas; zip, nix, natta!

When I realized that no one was talking for fear of losing their own job or causing another to lose his, I again met with the employees and promised them that no one would be involuntarily separated as a result of improvements in processes or systems.

Still, no one would talk, that is until the first man left for another job out of state.

We had already determined which positions were critical and would be retained and which positions were probably excess and could be eliminated. I knew that we had a normal annual turnover of 10% of the work force. The federally mandated process allowed for reductions in force to occur over a three-year period. Therefore, all we had to do was effect a hiring freeze for the next three years. As critical positions became vacant through normal attrition, we retrained people who were in non-critical positions. I explained all this to the employees but they still waited to see if we would follow through with what I had told them.

Then a machinist accepted a job at another installation out of state. We laterally moved a man from a non-critical position into this critical position and retrained him. That's when the floodgates burst open! Managers worked overtime trying to keep up with the pent up demand for innovation. Cycle time was drastically reduced, as were costs while innovative ideas long suppressed burst forth into the light of day.

When the fear of losing a job was removed, not by words alone but by actions, then and only then would the people actively and willingly participate in process improvement.

Forgiving mistakes. Do you remember whom it was that asked Jesus how many times should he forgive someone who has sinned against him? Oh, yes, it was Peter. The same Peter who the evening of His arrest proclaimed to Jesus that he would never deny Him and would even give up his life for Him. The same Peter who a few hours later denied three times even knowing Jesus. After His resurrection, Jesus found Peter hiding in Jerusalem in fear and shame and forgave him for his cowardice and betrayal (1 Corinthians 15:5). This same Peter would later be empowered by Jesus with the question, "Simon, son of Jonah, do you love me?" asked three times. Jesus knew Peter's heart and forgave him his weakness while charging him to "Feed my sheep" (John 21:15-17).

I enjoyed telling new staff officers during their welcome aboard interview that I *wanted* them to make mistakes. Usually, their eyes would roll around in their heads and I could see them thinking, "What, is this guy nuts! Mistakes! Making mistakes is the fastest way to finding yourself out on the street!"

Once their eyes began to refocus, I would explain that unless they were making mistakes, they were not trying new ideas. If they never made a mistake and just played it safe—stayed with the tried and true way of doing things—they would never be creative or innovative. And we would not get any better as an organization either.

Improving processes and systems entails making mistakes, trying some things that may not work out. "Just don't stay too long with the mistakes," I would counsel. "But I will never criticize you for trying a well-planned experiment that failed." "Keep trying and you will find a new path and it may likely lead outside the box!"

Peter thought he was being pretty magnanimous when he suggested to Jesus that he would be willing to forgive a brother who sinned against him up to *seven* times. Jesus replied,

"I do not say to you, up to seven times, but up to seventy times seven" (Matthew 18:22).

Jesus' answer makes it clear that we are to forgive those who sin against us an infinite number of times. When He was criticized for eating with tax collectors and sinners, He rebuked the self-righteous Pharisees with this challenge:

"But go and learn what this means: 'I desire

mercy and not sacrifice.'" (Matthew 9:13).

Even in the hour of His greatest need, His three closest friends could not stay awake to pray with Him. Yet He was mercifully forgiving:

> Then He came to the disciples and found them sleeping, and said to Peter, "What? Could you not watch with Me one hour? Watch and pray, lest you enter into temptation. The spirit indeed is willing, but the flesh is weak" (Matthew 26:40, 41).

Jesus' rebuke is mild recognizing that His three friends had good intentions but they were not able to follow through. They had a good plan but their execution was found lacking.

When a mistake occurs our tendency is to look for someone to blame. Deming reminds us that most mistakes are not the fault of people anyway. Most mistakes (about 85%) are due to the process. Only about 15% of the time are mistakes attributable to human error (Deming 1982). People perform their work under the direction of management. They use the materials purchased by management. They use the machines supplied by management. Management owns the process. People work *in* the process; i.e., within the rules and procedures established by management. Therefore, process errors belong to management. Management works *on* the process and must fix process errors. Shooting the messenger will not fix the problem. Breaking down the process and discovering the special causes for mistakes will.

Jesus used mistakes as opportunities to teach important lessons recognizing that we are most receptive when we are vulnerable. That morning by the Sea of Tiberias, Jesus was to use Peter's shame to teach him a lesson in leadership he would never forget. Reading between the lines, Jesus in essence said,

> "Peter, do you really love me even after you denied knowing me? Then, if you do, take the leadership role I have prepared for you and care for my followers."

Those who are placed in positions of leadership are charged to do likewise: to care for their followers. Caring for followers means encouraging risk taking and forgiving mistakes. Leaders must recognize the fallibility of human beings but be slow to point the finger. I am often reminded of Jesus' challenge:

> "He who is without sin among you, let him throw a stone at her first" (John 8:7).

> *"Tend the flock of God that is your charge, not by constraint but willingly, not for shameful gain but eagerly, not as domineering over those in our charge but being examples to the flock."*
>
> *—1 Peter 5:2, 3*

Jesus' Tactics Summarized

The tactics Jesus used to implement his five-phase strategy are applicable to all forms of organizations, both for-profit and not-for-profit. He prepared His future leadership team through direct one-on-one teaching and small group leadership development. His public teaching was crafted with stories and illustrations at the level and in the language of His audience. It was directed at building commitment to the organization and its guiding principles. He led by personal example. He prepared His disciples and then delegated to them responsibility, authority, and accountability. By His very presence, He drove out fear and anxiety and radiated a calm assurance. He encouraged risk-taking and used mistakes as an opportunity to teach and grow. His approach to leadership was as servant first.

In the following chapters we will examine the leadership style of two contemporary leaders who have successfully applied the concept of servant as leader.

16

And the Word Became Flesh

"For to everyone to whom much is given, from him much will be required; and to whom much has been committed, of him they will ask the more."
—*Luke 12:48*

Miraculously healed at age 10, his college education funded by a stranger, he felt God calling him to a life of ministry to the poor as a young teen. Today, he heads a global ministry among the poor and disenfranchised staffed entirely by twenty-somethings.

Born in Omaha, Nebraska, on December 11, 1971, Chris Heuertz is Executive Director of Word Made Flesh, a ministry serving among the poorest of the poor. Now head-quartered in Omaha, Word Made Flesh currently has two children's homes in Madras/Chennai, India. One of these homes serves severely mentally and physically disabled abandoned children. The other home's primary focus is pediatric AIDS care and was the first of its kind in South India. They have a concurrent ministry in India among destitute women many of whom are HIV positive, widowed, divorced, or victims of domestic violence, and among women struggling to escape lives of prostitution (C. Heuertz, personal communication, August-September 2000).

Chris is the oldest of six siblings in a family that includes two adopted children. His parents have always been hard-working and God-fearing examples to their family, often holding multiple jobs each to put food on the table and clothes on the backs of their growing family. His childhood was characterized by lots of affirmation and encouragement from his parents and strong family relationships.

At age ten Chris contracted viral spinal meningitis and encephalitis. He slipped into a coma and the doctors told his parents that there was only a 30% chance he would live. If he did recover, they were told, he would be blind, deaf, and paralyzed from the neck down. They began to pray and to petition God to let their son live. One day, their pastor, the Reverend Elmer Murdoch of Trinity Church, Omaha, stopped by to check on Chris' condition. He laid hands on Chris' comatose body and prayed. By the end of the prayer Chris had opened his eyes—he was completely healed! After a battery of astonished doctors confirmed that he showed no signs of the disease, Chris was released from the hospital.

As a rising sophomore in high school, Chris' mom encouraged him to go on a church-sponsored mission trip to a Navajo reservation. There God awakened Chris to the needs of the poor and he committed his life to Christ and in service to others. His conversion was so dramatic that others were drawn to him and his message and he spoke frequently at schools, churches, and to ministries helping the poor. He began a weekly Bible study at his home that attracted up to 70 teens that would come to hear the message of God's love, forgiveness, and service to others.

As he neared the end of high school, Chris felt strongly that the Lord was calling him to live his life completely for Him. He wanted to go to a college where he could study God's Word but he knew that his parents, although they encouraged him to go, were unable to fund his education.

Then God intervened.

As his family was leaving church one day, a stranger asked if he could have a ride downtown. Chris' father responded that they would take him wherever he needed to go and they dropped him at his hotel. As they pulled away from the hotel, Chris' mother turned to the children and reminded them that they should always be kind to strangers, "...for by so doing some have unwittingly entertained angels" (Hebrews 13:2).

The stranger called the next day and said he wanted to thank the family for their kindness and could he take them to dinner? Over the meal, the strangers began to know one another. He was a medical doctor from Texas, the new Senior Medical Director for Mutual of Omaha Insurance Company. He was in town looking for a home and church for his family who would be relocating soon from Southern California. This doctor and Chris began to spend time together and when his wife arrived, Chris was invited to dinner. After supper, the couple revealed to Chris that for several months they had been having a series of simultaneous dreams. When they awoke, one could fill in the details for the other. The last image they saw was of someone dipping a spear or sword into water and when the weapon was drawn from the water it was covered with fish. They told Chris that they believed that meeting him was a fulfillment of that vision. They asked if they could help him realize his calling by funding his college education.

Chris enrolled in Asbury College, Wilmore, Kentucky, the next fall. While a student, each semester Chris would enter into discipleship with 5 to 6 other students who would hold each other accountable during the formative college years. The summer before his graduation, Chris spent several months in Calcutta with Mother Teresa and the Missionaries of Charity. When he returned, he knew that his life needed to count for the poorest of the poor. He graduated in 1994 with a degree in Missiology and Theology and a minor in Ancient Biblical Languages.

In 1991, an itinerant evangelist and gifted speaker, Shane Clark, had founded Word Made Flesh in Georgia. Shane and Chris studied together for a year at Asbury College. When Chris joined the ministry after graduation their staff consisted of two people: Shane and Chris. It remained that way for the next two years. He was their first missionary to Madras, India, arriving with no job description, no expectations, and little financial support. Within three months, he brought together an Indian Board of Directors consisting of nine local church leaders, had hired staff, and had established the first Word Made Flesh home for HIV-infected children, abandoned babies and social orphans. This home became the first pediatric AIDS care home of its kind in South India. A second children's home was initiated in Madras, India, in the Fall of 1995. Shane stepped down in 1996 as Executive Director and Chris assumed leadership.

In addition to pioneering the Word Made Flesh home in South India, Chris has served as Field Director in India and as a coordinator for Servant Teams who spend up to six months among the poor in South Asia, Eastern Europe, and South America. He has traveled extensively through nearly 50 countries working among the poorest of the poor, gypsies, and children with AIDS in Romania, prostitutes and recovering drug addicts in Hong Kong, street children in South America, and unreached peoples in rural Ugandan villages.

Chris met Phileena at Asbury in February 1994, just three months before he was to graduate. They maintained a long-distance romance over the next two years and still have several hundred pages of letters to document their budding relationship. They married in April 1996 and Phileena joined Chris on the mission field. Today, they share administrative and pastoral duties for Word Made Flesh and spend an average of six to seven months each year overseas with staff and in ministry among the poor. Chris serves not only as the International and Executive Director but also as a pastor to the ministry community, and is a writer and teacher. He and Phileena travel extensively sharing what God has done in and through their lives bringing a prophetic message to the Church to return to God's standard for justice for the poor, righteousness, and holy living.

Chris feels that his life has been characterized by people investing in him and he wants to invest in others both by building community and through discipleship. Word Made Flesh reflects that vision. Today the ministry has a staff of nearly 100 people from North America, Nepal, Bolivia, India, Peru, and Romania serving in twelve countries—and none of them are over 30 years old!

How does Chris lead? He shuns the traditional organizational forms and prefers to develop relationships and community among his staff. "Lots of people have taken chances with me so I let people make mistakes. That's how you learn." He prefers to be thought of as a friend and brother rather than as a director. He pushes decisions down to the lowest level preferring in-country decisions to high-level pronouncements. Communication is critical and he works at communicating at different levels. He thinks of the staff as both friends and colleagues and works to maintain that duality. He observed in his mentors that their lives validated their word—they lived what they said—and he checks his integrity first before asking someone to do something. What is your vision, I asked? "To be a better husband," was his reply. "I want to learn more about freedom in my life and how being free frees others." The hard questions dealing with justice and injustice and how to intercede for the cause of the poor occupies his prayer life. The future is a little frightening for Chris. The ministry's growth since the fall of 1996 has been explosive. Yet he understands that this group of twenty-somethings can't control this work. His desire is to allow the Holy Spirit free reign with the ministry so that it will emerge in the evolving form dictated by Jesus. He wants to involve even younger people in the ministry and to do more economic development, childcare and rehabilitation all cradled in knowing the heart of God and His character. His desire is to use God's material provision to develop His kingdom.

Personally, he struggles with his own role. Should he be a writer, teacher, leader, revolutionary? He is drawn to all those roles yet his heart longs to be an intimate friend with the poor and not to be removed from those relationships.

Chris Heuertz is a servant first.

Other voices. How do others see Chris Heuertz as leader? The following are testimonies from others serving under Chris' leadership in their own words. They speak eloquently of his servanthood (B. Anderson, personal communication, August-September 2000).

Field Staff Member, Lima, Peru. "You want a *backbreaker*, Martin?

As he poses this playful question, Chris Heuertz simultaneously lifts the aloof, skinny Lima street teen up over his knee in a mock wrestling move. The slightly skeptical Martin breaks into a wide grin and within minutes he has bonded with Chris.

Chris Heuertz is a servant leader. He leads by example. As he and his wife Phileena walk in obedience to the call

God has placed on their lives to serve the poor, they draw others around them.

Whether he is giving a street teen a "back-breaker", leading a book discussion, sharing his heart over a meal, or encouraging his staff, Chris is always in a posture of service. This humble posture allows him to empower others to ask the hard questions he himself is grappling with.

Chris is willing to allow others to see how he is also growing into his calling to serve the poor. His honesty, openness and friendship encourage others to seek God's heart for the poor and for reconciliation with the Church.

Acting Nepal Field Director, Katmandu, Nepal. Chris possesses an unusual quality given his position among us: when I am with him I feel as if he is truly AMONG us, not OVER us. I have felt that he does not take any particular personal glory in the fact that he is the director but simply sees it as a position from which to uniquely serve.

Future Servant Team Coordinator, La Paz, Bolivia. As I look at the nature of Word Made Flesh I see a correlation between Chris' leadership and that of the mission. Chris is a servant leader. He is a person that doesn't look at numbers or productivity but rather he possesses a Biblical understanding of how we are to live our lives. This means denial of our selfish desires and a more intentional approach to the needs of others.

As I spent time with Chris I would say that I learned more from watching him than from talking with him. I witnessed Chris giving of his time and energy to those who have so little. I will never forget the day he took us to visit a young girl who was living in the back of a restaurant with her six-month-old baby in Lima, Peru. My eyes were opened to the cry of the poor and my heart continues to break when I think of her.

Staff Members, Peru. Early on we were aware of Chris' ability to persuade people with both his speaking gifts and his personal convictions. The unique quality Chris possesses is the integration between his point of view and his actions. One example that stands out to us is when we were traveling with Chris and Phileena to Peru and they were bumped up to first class seating. The other members of the team were to be seated in coach. Chris and Phileena changed our tickets to first class and they took the coach tickets! This small act of service shone brightly in our hearts when we realized that our leader cared more for us than he did himself.

Advocacy Coordinator. Chris has a remarkable gift for bringing out the giftedness of others often when they don't see these gifts in themselves. I believe this is the mark of a true leader. Chris' focus is not on how he can exert power or authority over others but rather how he can nurture the lives of others.

Servant Team Coordinator, Peru. His innovativeness, vision, and incredible work ethic have caused Word Made Flesh to mature and grow as an international community. Though he is my age, I consider him my mentor. Through our friendship Chris' leadership style has given me freedom to explore my strengths as well as guide me with encouragement and wise counsel.

Word Made Flesh Board Member. I see in Chris a friend and a leader who seeks to know and identify with a God whose authority and kingship comes from a place of humility and brokenness. He has rejected the belief that leadership is based on position and power and instead has bent his knees in the position of a servant. When you are with Chris there is no doubt that he is a man of deep conviction and far reaching influence that find their source in the life-giving presence of Jesus. Because Chris is a receptor and a learner he leads by lifting others up. He leads by serving just as Jesus did.

Administrative Staff. Chris has extraordinary gifts in a

number of areas: persuasive public speaker, skilled disciplinarian, math wiz, visionary, incredible memory, and gifted with languages. And yet he is teachable, vulnerable, and intentional and has a great love for children. These traits do not normally come together in one person. They are almost paradoxical.

Phileena Heuertz. Chris has many roles: prophet, revolutionary, critical thinker, and friend of the poor. But it is his servant's heart that drives him in each of these roles. He routinely sacrifices his needs and self-interests for the sake of others. Probably the most powerful example of servant leadership is found in his love for the poor and oppressed. He loves them with the passion of Christ. Although he is the leader of a growing ministry he takes no pride in position but prefers the humble seat among the poor, particularity the children.

17

To Set the Captives Free

"I was in prison, and you came to Me."
—Matthew 25:36

"I am also bound by the Father's will. There are many
things pleasurable to me that I may not do, even those
things that in themselves are ethically acceptable. I also am
bound by my brother's needs; I must go beyond the appeal-
ing ideology of socialism: 'If anyone is hungry, I am
hungry; if anyone is cold, I am cold; if anyone is in prison,
I am not free.'"
—W. Glyn Evans

He is a natural resources attorney who deals with that most precious of Western U.S. resources—water. But he recognized a calling to a more important resource—people. Now he volunteers his time to assist undocumented aliens seeking political asylum in the United States for fear of persecution in their native country.

He was born to a cotton farming family where both parents set an example for their children of service to community and others. He was a successful lawyer, Chairman of the Arizona Republican Caucus and on his way to a career in politics when his life journey took an unexpected turn.

Richard Neely Morrison was born in 1947 in Gilbert, Arizona. The oldest of three boys, his early childhood was spent in relative poverty. By the time he had turned six the family income had improved and yet those values of hard work and personal responsibility learned on the farm were firmly ingrained. These values would shape his future career and vocational choices. His father's financial success led him to believe that with hard work anyone could achieve their monetary goals. Only later did he realize that this was not true for everyone even in a wealthy country like the United States. (R. Morrison, personal communication, June 2003).

In his small town life revolved around the church and school. His childhood was molded by good old-fashioned Methodist values of zeal, enthusiasm, selflessness and service to others. His parents were active in the community and the church where his mother served as the church organist for 38 years. They sang in the choir, taught Sunday School, and led the Youth program. His father served on the local school board and on 35 different local and state boards and commissions. It was also in that church that he was introduced to Boy Scouts and the values inherent to scouting, eventually he became an Eagle Scout.

In high school he learned the importance of teamwork, goal-setting, and humility through sports where he excelled at football and track. Basketball taught him the limits of his gifts and abilities. Valedictorian of his small high school graduating class, he was on his way to college and pursuit of the American dream.

An uncle, John Sawyer, had a profound impact on his life, which he realized only years later. Richard believes Uncle John was the first man in their community to go away to college and earn admission to Phi Beta Kappa. Later John Sawyer served as superintendent of schools. He also ran a family farm—a task at which he was not particularly successful, at least not financially. But Richard noticed that his uncle chose to put people ahead of business in everything he did. While others were critical of him as a businessman, John Sawyer chose to be a servant. He was always there for whoever was in need even when it meant he would suffer personally or professionally. This was a lesson that young Richard would carry with him to maturity. When Richard's first child was born, John Sawyer and his wife arrived at the hospital even before Richard's own parents!

In 1967, while a sophomore at Northern Arizona University, Richard received word that his father had been severely injured in an automobile accident. His father would recover from this near-death experience but the physical and psychological trauma resulting from the accident eventually ended his father's public service. It also had a lasting effect upon Richard and helped to shape his leadership style. This formative experience taught him that bad things do happen to good people and that all families struggle with pain. As a young man he recognized for the first time that leaders must be sensitive to the needs of others and that an important role for a leader is as a hope-giver.

Following graduation, Richard joined the Navy and served for six years as a fighter pilot and then ROTC instructor at Rice University. Over time he began to chafe at the command and control model of leadership he experienced in the Navy. He began to lose interest in a naval career and turned to the law to fulfill his life's ambitions. Inspired by the concept that people should set their sights on transcendent ideals and a growing realization that a naval career would not be compatible with his highest values, he attended law school at night while he taught ROTC classes by day. Graduating from the University of Houston Law School in 1977, he set his sights on a legal career of service to others.

Richard first sensed a call to ordained ministry while in college but this call became clearer in law school. However, his wife did not share that same vision and his call was deferred. He began to look for other ways to serve the community. While starting a new career as a lawyer, he was involved in the family farming business and became quickly immersed in civic and charitable activities. At the same time, he obtained a local license to preach and within a few years had served in virtually every position within the local church.

During the mid-1980's he served as Chairman of the Arizona Republican Caucus and pictured himself as a future congressman. But then as he looked at those around him who were striving for power and position he began to realize that the most contented, most fulfilled, best people he knew were those from his farm experience. They were the ones who truly led an abundant life with less stress and more time for people. He decided he needed to get off the "ego track" and get "authentic." At the same time the law began to lose its appeal to him, which he increasingly saw as oriented toward self-preservation. He took a leave of absence from his law practice and enrolled in the Graduate Theological Union in Berkley, California. It took several years to finish that seminary education as he returned to his law practice to support his wife and daughters. Eventually he was ordained a deacon in the Episcopal Church USA.

Life experiences have molded Richard's leadership style. His early leadership was crisp, energetic, focused, purposeful, structured and hierarchical. Over time he realized that the command and control model is not the best approach to leading people toward their highest good. He believes that the human asset is the most underutilized asset in America today. Therefore open access to information and visioning which empowers people through cooperation are much more effective leadership approaches. He began to see that Jesus was not interested in just words; he wanted behaviors that affirmed people.

Today he leads by building relationships, by encouraging others. He is critical of behaviors that are self-seeking and ego-driven. He works to build people up instead of tearing them down. He practices life style modeling and offers his life as an example of what it means to be committed to the common good and to the encouragement and uplifting of every single person. He is critical of what he calls "intellectual snobbery" without being critical of the intellectual. He has confronted the principalities and powers and the choices he has made have defied conventional cultural assumptions. His lifestyle is characterized by voluntary and deliberate downward mobility. He recognizes the value, worth and dignity of each individual and that "what I am is not necessarily what I do."

His interests are many and varied. Following in his father's footsteps, he currently serves on 22 boards and commissions. His public and charitable service extends back over 20 years when he helped form an institute of public policy at Arizona State University. He continues to serve on that board. His retiring address to the Arizona Republican Caucus was on the importance of grounding public service in religious values. He serves on the board of the Institute of Servant Leadership and the national board of the American Agricultural Law Association. His interests extend to higher education where he served as vice president of the School of Theology at Claremont and taught part-time at the Morrison School of Agribusiness and Resource Management at Arizona State University.

The dominant leadership trait in Richard Morrison's life

is his understanding that his service is a faithful response to the love and activity of God in his life. (We learned to love because God first loved us.) This requires a certain consciousness, an awareness of our motivation for service: is it driven by ego or a genuine desire to serve others? Other important traits include being self-disciplined and self-motivated, understood in the context of a faithful response to God's activity in his life.

These traits were developed over time and as a result of life experiences. With maturity, he began to understand that God's grace offers beauty, love, forgiveness, compassion, encouragement, and vision even when we don't deserve any of them. However he understands that experiential learning can imprison us particularly after a negative or failing experience. Only through the lens of a mature, spiritual perspective can we rise above and essentially reject the negative lessons of a failing experience. This required lots of prayer and reflection on his part. In time he concluded that life is supposed to be an affair of the heart based on love of God and love of neighbor.

As a natural resources attorney he lives in a world of tension. He is confronted daily with people who wish to promote their own good, often at the expense of others. He tries to guide litigants to see beyond their own self-interest and to seek reconciliation. He has found that empathetic listening is an effective way of guiding people toward reordering the values and reprioritizing their goals.

His home State of Arizona has rather porous borders and growing up on a farm Richard was no stranger to illegal immigrants. In the mid-1990's he was introduced to refugees seeking political asylum in the United States due to their fear of persecution if they were returned home. Knowing that desperate people would say what they think he wanted to hear, he would ask for evidence of persecution in order to screen out those with creative imaginations.

He learned to brace himself before their shirts came up. With direct, physical evidence (e.g., scars, burns, missing limbs) it was easy to agree to represent those most needy refugees before the Immigration Court. He is undefeated over the last six years in representing undocumented aliens who are seeking asylum.

Since 1997, Richard Morrison has focused on serving the needs of the most vulnerable in his community. That is the mark of a servant leader. His extraordinary journey in pursuit of overarching ideas has taken him from an Arizona cotton farm to become a Navy fighter pilot, lawyer, politico, deacon and advocate for the persecuted.

He responded to a life-long calling in June 2003 when he entered full-time ministry as a priest in the Episcopal Church.

References

Ackerson, L. (1942). *Children's Behavior Problems: Relative Importance and Intercorrelations Among Traits.* Chicago: University of Chicago Press.

American Society for Quality (2000). *W. Edwards Deming: A mission pursued on two continents.* http://www.asq.org/about/history/deming.html (6/12/00).

Barna, G. (1998). *The Second Coming of the Church.* Nashville, TN: Thomas Nelson.

Bass, B.M. (1985). *Leadership and Performance beyond Expectations.* New York: Free Press.

Bennis, W.G. (1992). *Leaders on Leadership.* Boston: Harvard Business Review Books.

Bennis, W. and B. Nanus. (1985). *Leaders, The Strategies for Taking Command.* New York: Harper & Row.

Bird, C. (1940). *Social Psychology.* New York: Appleton.

Blake, R.R., and A.A. McCanse. (1991). *Leadership Dilemmas—Grid Solutions.* Houston, TX: Gulf.

Bray, D.W., and D.L. Grant (1966). Predicting organizational effectiveness with a four-factor theory of leadership. *Psychological Monographs* 80(17): No. 625.

Bradley, J., and R. Powers. (2000). *Flags of our Fathers.* New York: Bantam Books.

Burns, J.M. (1978). *Leadership.* New York: Harper & Row.

Carlyle, T. [1841] (1907). *Heroes and Hero Worship.* Boston: Adams.

Clark, D. (1996). Microsoft Creates New Executive Group, Realigns Duties of Two Star Managers. *Wall Street Journal.* C-12: December 4, 1996.

Collopy, M. (1996). *Works of Love are Works of Peace.* San Francisco: Ignatius Press.

Conger, J.A. (1991). Inspiring others: The language of leadership. *Academy of Management Executive* 5(1):31-45.

Covey, S. R. (1989). *The Seven Habits of Highly Effective People.* New York: Simon and Schuster.

Covey, S. R. (1990). *Principle-Centered Leadership.* New York: Fireside.

Covey, S., R.A. Merrill, and R.R. Merrill. (1994). *First Things First.* New York: Simon & Schuster.

Crocker III, H.W. (1999). *Robert E. Lee on Leadership.* Rocklin, CA: Prima Publishing.

Deming, W. E. (1982). *Out of the Crisis.* Cambridge, MA: Center for Advanced Engineering Study, MIT.

Deming, W.E. (2000). *The New Economics, For Industry, Government, Education.* 2nd Ed. Cambridge, MA: The MIT Press.

Deming, W. E. (1988). Presented at a Deming five-day seminar.

DePree, M. (1989) *Leadership is an Art.* New York: Doubleday.

DePree, M. (1992). *Leadership Jazz.* New York: Dell Publishing.

Eldredge, J. (2003). *Walking the Dead, The Glory of a Heart Fully Alive.* Nashville: Thomas Nelson Publishers.

Elton Mayo's Hawthorne Experiments. (2000). http://www. accel-team.com/motivation/hawthorne_02.html (6/12/00).

Evans, W.G. (1979). *Daily with the King.* Chicago: The Moody Bible Institute.

Fiedler, F.E. (1967). *A Theory of Leadership Effectiveness.* New York: McGraw-Hill.

Ford, L. (1991). *Transforming Leadership.* Downers Grove, IL: InterVarsity Press.

Galton, F. (1869). Hereditary genius. *Hereditary Genius.* New York: Appleton.

Glasgow Quaker Meeting (1995). *Quaker Business Meetings: How Friends Make Decisions.* http://www.gla.ac.uk/~gkea04/business.html#Overview (9/17/00).

Goodman, A.J. (2000). *The National Survey on Public Leadership: Abridged Results.* Boulder, CO: Student Leadership Institute.

Graham, B. (1997). *Just As I Am: The Autobiography of Billy Graham.* New York: HarperSanFrancisco (Zondervan).

Greenleaf, R. K. (1977). *Servant Leadership: A journey into the nature of legitimate power and greatness.* New York: Paulist Press.

Hayford, J.W. (Ed.). (1991). Map 1: The Nations of Genesis 10. *Spirit Filled Life Bible.* Nashville: Thomas Nelson Publishers.

Hemphill, J.K. (1949). The Leader and His Group. *Journal of Educational Research* 28:225-229, 245-246.

Hersey, P., and K.H. Blanchard. (1969). Life Cycle Theory of Leadership. *Training and Development Journal* 23:26-34.

Hersey, P., and K.H. Blanchard. (1977). *Management of Organizational Behavior: Utilizing Human Resources.* 3rd ed., Englewood Cliffs, NJ: Prentice Hall.

Hersey, P., and K.H. Blanchard. (1982). *Management of Organizational Behavior: Utilizing Human Resources.* 4th ed., Englewood Cliffs, NJ: Prentice Hall.

Hersey, P., K.H. Blanchard, and D.E. Johnson. (2001). *Management of Organizational Behavior: Leading Human Resources.* 8th ed., Upper Saddle River, NJ: Prentice Hall.

Hesse, H. (1956). *The Journey to the East.* New York: The Noonday Press.

Hughes, R. L, R.C. Ginnett, and G.J. Curphy. (1993). *Leadership, Enhancing the Lessons of Experience.* Homewood, IL.

Hunter, G.G.III. (2000). *The Celtic Way of Evangelism.* Nashville: Abingdon Press.

James, W. (1880). Great men, great thoughts and their environment. *Atlantic Monthly* 46:441-459.

Janis, I.L. (1983). *Groupthink.* 2nd Ed. Boston: Houghton Mifflin.

Jenkins, W.O. (1947) A review of leadership studies with particular reference to military problems. *Psychological Bulletin* 44:54-79.

Johnson, R. S. (1993). *Leadership for the Quality Transformation.* Milwaukee: ASQC Quality Press.

Jones, L. B. (1995). *Jesus CEO: Using Ancient Wisdom for Visionary Leadership.* New York: Hyperion.

Juran, J. M. (1989). *Juran on Leadership for Quality.* New York: The Free Press.

Kouzes, J.M., and B.Z. Posner. (1993). *Credibility: How Leaders Gain and Lose It, Why People Demand It.* San Francisco: Jossey-Bass.

Laan, R.V. (1996). *Echoes of His Presence.* Colorado Springs, CO: Focus on the Family Publishing.

Lewin, K., and R. Lippit. (1938). An experimental approach to the study of autocracy and democracy: A preliminary note. *Sociometry* 1:292-300.

Lewin, K., R. Lippit, and R.K. White. (1939). Patterns of aggressive behavior in experimentally created social climates. *Journal of Social Psychology* 10:271-301.

Likert, R. (1961). *New Patterns of Management.* New York: McGraw-Hill.

Lord, R.G., C.L. DeVader, and G.M. Allinger. (1986). A Meta-Analysis of the Relationship between Personality

Traits and Leadership Perceptions: An Application of Validity Generalization Procedures. *Journal of Applied Psychology* 71:402-410.

Mann, R.D. (1959). A review of the Relationships between Personality and Performance in Small Groups. *Psychological Bulletin* 56:241-270.

Map 1, The Nations of Genesis 10 (1983). *Spirit Filled Life Bible*, New King James Edition. Nashville: Thomas Nelson Publishers.

Maxwell, J. C. (1995). *Developing the Leaders Around You.* Nashville: Thomas Nelson.

McClelland, D.C. (1962). Business Drive and National Achievement. *Harvard Business Review,* July-August:99-112.

McGregor, D. (1966). *Leadership and Motivation.* Cambridge, MA: MIT Press.

Nair, K. (1994). *A Higher Standard of Leadership, Lessons from the Life of Gandhi.* San Francisco: Berrett-Koehler.

Nahavandi, Afsaneh. (2000). *The Art and Science of Leadership.* Upper Saddle River, New Jersey: Prentice Hall.

Noonan, P. (2001). *When Character was King.* New York: Viking.

Oster, M.J. (1991). *Vision-Driven Leadership.* San Bernardino, CA: Here's Life Publishers.

Ott, E.R. (1967). *Tribute to Walter A. Shewhart.* http://www.asq.org/about/history/shewhart.html (6/12/00)

Packer, J. I. (1995). *A Passion for Faithfulness, Wisdom From the Book of Nehemiah.* Wheaton, IL: Crossway Books.

Peters, T. J. and R.H. Waterman, Jr. (1982). *In Search of Excellence.* New York: Warner Books.

Phillips, D. T. (1994). *Lincoln on Leadership, Executive Strategies for Tough Times.* New York: Warner Books.

Puryear, E.F., Jr. (1971). *19 Stars: A Study in Military*

Character and Leadership. Novato, CA: Presidio Press.

Roach, C.F., and O. Behling. (1984). Functionalism: Basis for an Alternate Approach to the Study of Leadership. *Leaders and Managers: International Perspectives on Managerial Behavior and Leadership.* New York: Pergamon.

Robert K. Greenleaf Center for Servant Leadership. (1996). *Who Was Robert K. Greenleaf?* http://www.greenleaf.org/rkgbio.html (6/15/00).

Roberts, W. (1990). *The Leadership Secrets of Attila the Hun.* New York: Warner Books.

Rychlak, J.F. (1963). Personality correlates of leadership among first level managers. *Psychological Reports* 12:43-52.

Sanders, J. O. (1994). *Spiritual Leadership.* Chicago: Moody Press.

Senge, P. M. (1990). *The Fifth Discipline: the art and practice of the learning organization.* New York: Doubleday.

Senge, P. M. (1990). The Leader's New Work. Printed in Sashkin, M, and K.J. Kiser. (1993). *Putting Total Quality Management to Work: What TQM Means, How to Use It & How to Sustain It over the Long Run.* San Francisco: Berrett-Koehler.

Shaara, M. (1974). *The Killer Angels.* New York: Ballantine Books,

Stogdill, R.M. (1948) Personal factors associated with leadership: A survey of the literature. *Journal of Psychology* 25:35-71.

Stogdill, R.M. (1974). *Handbook on Leadership.* 1st ed. New York: Free Press.

Tichy, N. M. and M.A. Devanna. (1986). *The Transformational Leader.* New York: John Wiley & Sons.

Tuchman, B.W. (1985). *March of Folly: From Troy to*

Vietnam. New York: Ballantine Books.

Vines, W. E. (1997). *Vine's Expository Dictionary of Old & New Testament Words.* Nashville: Thomas Nelson.

Walton, M. (1986). *The Deming Management Method.* New York: Putnam.

Walton, M. (1990). *Deming Management at Work.* New York: Putnam.

Webster's New Collegiate Dictionary (1961). Springfield, MA: G.&C. Merriam Company.

Wiersma, K., and B. Larson. (1997). *Fourteen Days in October: The Cuban Missile Crisis.* http://ww.library. advanced.org/11046 (7/1/00).

Wilkinson, B.H. (1994). *Teaching With Style.* Atlanta, GA: Walk Through the Bible Ministries.

Wilson, I. (1996). *Highlights of the Undisputed History.* http://www.shroud.com/history.html (7/1/00).

Wilson, I. (1998). *The Blood and the Shroud: New Evidence That the World's Most Sacred Relic Is Real.* New York: The Free Press.

CPSIA information can be obtained
at www.ICGtesting.com
Printed in the USA
LVOW11s1511101116

512464LV00002B/170/P